The Harriman Expedition to Alaska

The Harriman Expedition to Alaska

Encountering the Tlingit and Eskimo in 1899

GEORGE BIRD GRINNELL

with introductions by
Polly Burroughs and Victoria Wyatt

University of Alaska Press
Fairbanks

P.O. Box 756240
Fairbanks, AK 99775-6240

ISBN 978-1-889963-98-3 (paperback)

Publisher's Note

The final report of the Harriman Expedition was published in eleven volumes from 1901 to 1905. The essays by George Bird Grinnell are reprinted here with their original page numbers as they appeared in volumes 1 and 2. Two color plates from the original are reproduced in black and white.

Library of Congress Cataloging-in-Publication Data

Grinnell, George Bird, 1849–1938.
The Harriman expedition to Alaska : encountering the Tlingit and Eskimo in 1899 / George Bird Grinnell ; with introductions by Polly Burroughs and Victoria Wyatt.
p. cm.
These essays are reprinted with original page numbers as they appeared in v. 1 and 2 of the final report of the Harriman Expedition published from 1901 to 1905.
Includes bibliographical references and index.

ISBN 978-1-889963-98-3 (pbk. : alk. paper)

1. Eskimos—Alaska—Social life and customs. 2. Tlingit Indians—Alaska—Social life and customs. 3. Salmon fishing—Alaska. 4. Alaska—Social life and customs. 5. Alaska—Description and travel. 6. Harriman Alaska Expedition (1899) I. Title.
E99.E7G817 2007
979.8004'971—dc22 2006100120

Printed in the United States

This publication was printed on paper that meets the minimum requirements for ANSI/NISO Z39.48–1992 (Permanence of Paper).

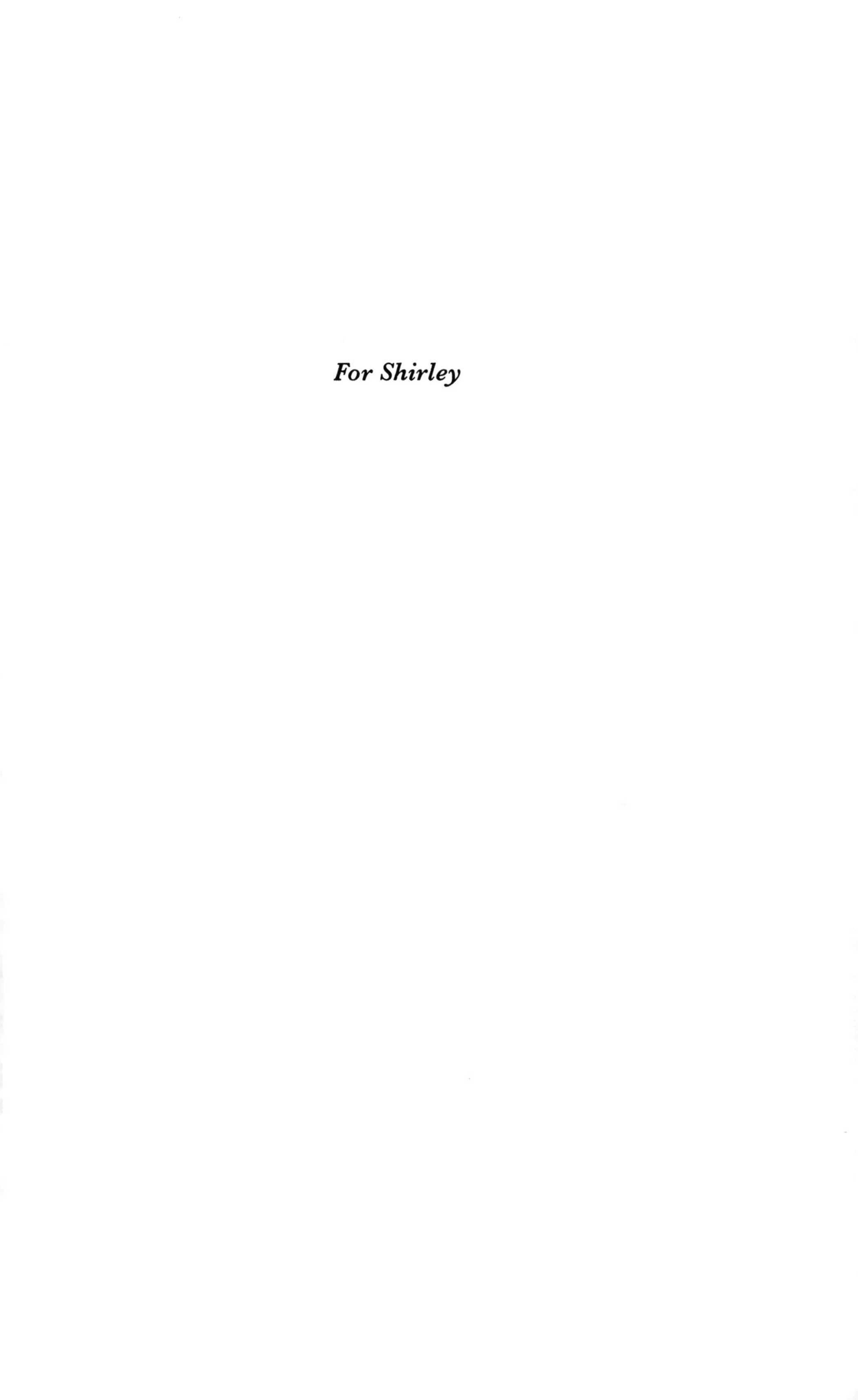

For Shirley

CONTENTS

Painting by F. S. Dellenbaugh. Lith. Taber-Prang Art Co.

POPOF STRAIT, SHUMAGIN ISLANDS.

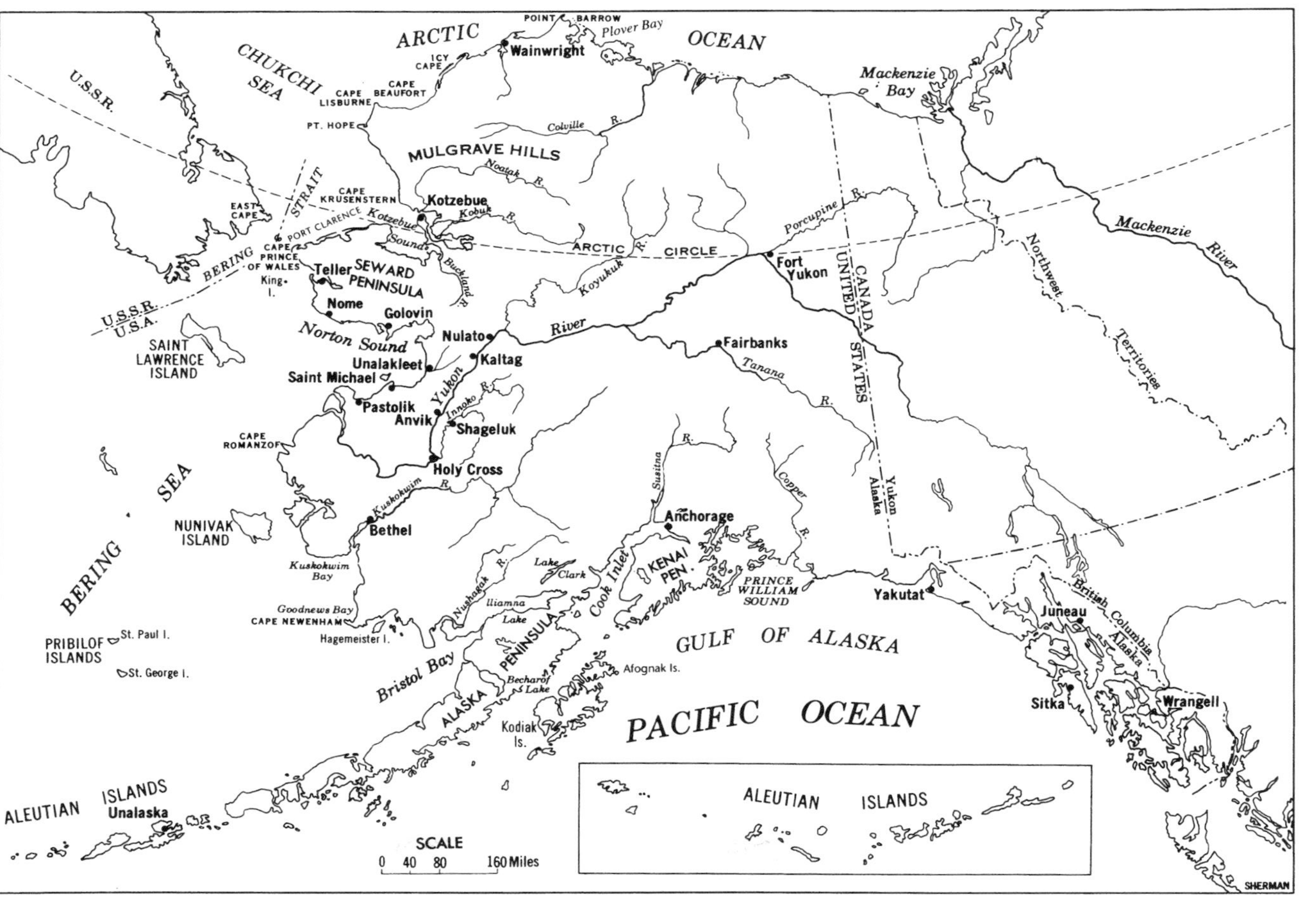

MAP I. The Coast of Alaska

MAP 2. Southeast Alaska

Introductions

George Bird Grinnell in his New York office, ca. 1920.

GEORGE BIRD GRINNELL, PIONEER CONSERVATIONIST

by POLLY BURROUGHS

Mr. Grinnell, I am struck by the fact that this year I have the pleasure of presenting these Roosevelt medals to three pioneers. You and Miss Berry and Governor Pinchot have all been trailblazers. In the case of Miss Berry and Mr. Pinchot, however, it is true only in a figurative sense.

But you were with General Custer in the Black Hills and with Colonel Ludlow in the Yellowstone. You lived among the Indians; you became a member of the Blackfoot tribe. Your studies of their language and customs are authoritative. Few men have done so much as you, none has done more to preserve the vast areas of picturesque wilderness for the eyes of posterity in the simple majesty in which you and your fellow pioneers first beheld them.

In Yellowstone you prevented the exploitation, and therefore the destruction, of the natural beauty. The Glacier National Park is peculiarly your monument.

As editor for thirty-five years of a journal devoted to outdoor life, you have done a noteworthy service in bringing to the men and women of a hurried and harried age the relaxation and revitalization which come from contact with nature. I am glad to have a part in the public recognition which your self-effacing and effective life has won.

PRESIDENT CALVIN COOLIDGE, PRESENTING THE THEODORE ROOSEVELT DISTINGUISHED SERVICE MEDAL TO GRINNELL, EAST ROOM OF THE WHITE HOUSE, 1925

The Industrial Revolution was at its peak at the turn of the century. It was an era of spectacular growth and creativity in manufacturing, mining, the fishing and fur trades, shipping, and westward expansion. Any grandiose venture was considered possible: the Suez Canal, the Panama Canal, the Eiffel Tower, a transcontinental railroad, the Brooklyn Bridge, and the telephone talking wire — a golden age in America before income tax and after plumbing.

Hunting, fishing, and sightseeing tours to the West and to Alaska, the country's newest frontier, had become very popular with the nation's wealthy. The Pacific Steamship Company's cruises along the coast were doing a flourishing business. Prized big-game trophies adorned the libraries of New York townhouses, and the stories behind the skin rugs on the floors were a favorite topic of conversation at elegant dinner parties.

Edward H. Harriman, a business magnate of this colorful period, had left school for Wall Street when he was fourteen years old and had become an enormously successful investor and railroad baron, who nevertheless was considered an outsider by Wall Street's elite. A clergyman's son with little education, he was shrewd, rough-hewn, and socially unacceptable. Always searching for new business ventures, he decided to organize and finance a scientific expedition along the Alaska coast. The proposed trip would include scientists, artists, photographers, and taxidermists. He envisioned this floating university as a grand philanthropic gesture that would gain him credibility in New York's social and business circles and, in addition, enable him to investigate the possibility of a railroad under the Bering Strait and around the world. Why not? he reasoned. Not unmindful of the economic potential of the vast, virgin wilderness with its oil, gold, copper, and furs, he would see for himself; and he would shroud the plan in his unique scientific experiment. Of almost equal importance was his determination to shoot a large Alaskan brown bear like those he had seen in the trophy rooms of other sportsmen.

He purchased an old iron steamship, the *Elder*, and had it fitted as a luxury liner with scientific labs and offices for the two-month cruise along the Alaska coast. C. Hart Merriam, chief of the U.S. Biological Survey, was asked to assemble the expedition group while the vessel was in drydock in Seattle, being readied for the cruise. He chose many of his team from the inner circles of the Cosmos Club in Washington, D. C., and the National Academy of Sciences. There were to be 126 people in all, including the officers and crew of the vessel, the scientists, packers, camp hands and Harriman's own entourage of his wife, five children, three relatives, and a friend.

The group was treated to a cross-county sightseeing tour on Harriman's private train. The five luxurious "palace cars" offered delicious food and the finest cigars and included one car with an entire library of books on Alaska. After several stops along the way, the group arrived in Seattle and boarded ship, leaving port on the evening of May 31, 1899.

Among those who agreed to join the expedition were John Burroughs, ornithologist and author; Grove Karl Gilbert, a student of glaciers; Alaska explorer John Muir; artists R. Swain Gifford, Frederick S. Dellenbaugh, and Louis Agassiz Fuertes; Edward S. Curtis, who later became the country's foremost photographer of the Indians in the West; Henry Gannett, chief geographer of the U.S. Geological Survey; and George Bird Grinnell, ethnologist, author of books about American Indians, and publisher of *Forest and Stream* magazine. Never had such a large group of American scholars been assembled for an extended scientific cruise. With his keen organizational ability, Harriman himself planned many of the details for the group's creature comforts, from the fine food to the crystal champagne goblets. And Merriam, with his academic background, organized lectures that provoked spirited exchanges of ideas and philosophies to while away the long evening hours.

From geologist to ornithologist, each scientist pursued his particular discipline, leaving footprints from Seattle to Port Clarence in Norton Sound, a way station for the American whaling fleet going into the Arctic Ocean. The *Elder* cruised along the Alaskan coastline, dropping anchor at every spot that some member of the group wanted to explore. Depending upon the location, various among them would go ashore and camp for a few days to gather fossils, live specimens, dead birds, flora, fauna, and other scientific data or to hunt, fish, paint, and photograph. The group explored the spectacular, looming glaciers, the Eskimo and Indian camps and villages, and the copper mines; investigated the salmon industry and the fur trade's sealing and wolf industries; and observed the whaling offshore. Evenings were spent listening to lectures and making reports.

The Expedition experienced monotonous days at sea, foul weather, and boredom. Nevertheless, Harriman abounded with enthusiasm and curiosity and often rowed ashore with members of his family or romped on deck with his children. The scientists gathered mountains of material to study and eventually, in many cases, to give to various museums around the country. But it had been a long voyage, and by the time the vessel put into Port Clarence, many were anxious to return home. Harriman's announcement that he would have first pick of all the photographs that had been taken on the trip and would review all the text for his proposed two-volume, leather-bound account of the expedition, annoyed the group. Even Harriman had had enough; he missed the excitement, the shrewd, high-risk dealmaking of the New York business world. He exclaimed to Merriam, "I don't give a damn if I never see any more scenery."[1]

1. Goetzmann and Sloan, *Looking Far North*, p. 152.

Although the trip had led him to abandon the idea of a railroad tunnel under the Bering Strait, at least for the moment, he finally got his bear on Kodiak Island. The skin was not as big as some he had seen in New York parlors, and he had needed help in shooting the bear, but it was a trophy nevertheless.

When the *Elder* docked in Seattle on July 30, the press and hundreds of curious onlookers were there praising Harriman for this extraordinary venture. By their accounts it was an enormous success and made an invaluable contribution to the understanding of the country's newest frontier. The cruise had given its sponsor credibility in New York social and business circles, but his reputation was not to last. Soon enough he was again immersed in his often-questionable business dealings.

Because of his years of work with the Indians of the West, George Bird Grinnell's assignment for the trip was to report on the salmon industry and the Eskimos and Indians. The expedition team had observed the mining, fishing, and fur-taking operations; and, although Harriman viewed the Alaska natives as little more than cheap labor for these industries, Grinnell had been appalled at the conditions he saw. Wanton abuse and waste in the salmon industry had prompted him to write in his report, "The same language will be used that was heard in past years with regard to the abundance of wild pigeons, or of the buffalo, or of the fur seals of the Bering Sea." And of the Indians and Eskimos, whose ways of life had been so disrupted, he noted that "until the white man came and changed all their life, they lived well."[2] He frequently disagreed with the ethnologists whom he saw as primarily concerned with the reformation of the

2. Grinnell, *The Harriman Alaska Expedition*.

Indians and the Eskimos to the "American way" of language, religion, and work ethic.

Grinnell enjoyed John Muir's company in particular, but could not support Muir's notion that there should be no economic benefit to the rest of the nation from Alaska. The shy Scotsman felt the wilderness should be left untouched, while Grinnell had been advocating regulating its use with laws to protect and replenish the natural life cycles of fish, wildlife, and forests.

Explorers from Russia, Britain, the United States, and France had invaded the wilderness and had been rapacious in their use of its natural resources. It was not the idea of some development; it was the abuses that troubled Grinnell. Not only was he angered by the careless decimation of the fur seal, salmon, and sea otter, as well as the herd of reindeer also vital to the Native American's way of life (just as he had been about the buffalo of the Plains many years earlier), he was deeply concerned about Alaska's future (just as he had earlier been about the West's). Writing many monographs, articles for *Forest and Stream*, and books about American Indians, he had devoted years to helping form and pass legislation. He had begun addressing these problems twenty-five years earlier, when he was a graduate student at Yale University. Not content to concentrate on a single discipline and always looking at the broad picture, he wanted to work on many areas of conservation and their interrelationships.

Born in Brooklyn, New York, in 1849, to a wealthy, influential family, George Bird Grinnell was the eldest of George Blake and Helen Lansing's six children. The Grinnells were of Huguenot stock, and the first member of the family to arrive in America was Matthew, who left his father's chateau ("Pimont") in Burgundy for Rhode Island in 1630. He settled in Portsmouth, Rhode Island, on upper Narragansett Bay.

For the next three centuries subsequent generations of Grinnells distinguished themselves in education, politics, and business. George Bird was related to several Colonial governors and presidents of Yale University. His maternal ancestry included his great-great-grandfather Abram Jacob Lansing, the Dutch patroon of Lansingburgh, New York. The Auburn Theological Seminary in Auburn, New York, was founded by his grandfather, the Reverend Dirck C. Lansing. A paternal branch of the family, emanating from New Bedford, Massachusetts, included the owners of the Grinnell and Minturn Line, one of the largest and most successful shipping houses of the nineteenth century, which owned the famous clipper ship *Flying Cloud*.

George Bird's father, George Blake, was a successful textile merchant and, later, investment banker. One of eight children, George Blake was born and raised in Greenfield, Massachusetts, where his father practiced law and served in Congress along with Daniel Webster. Soon after he married, George Blake moved to New York City, where he worked for a cousin in the textile business. After several moves in the area, in 1857 he finally settled his growing family in Audubon Park, where he eventually built a large Victorian house — "The Hemlocks." He bought land from Lucy Audubon, widow of naturalist John Jay Audubon. The naturalist had been dead for six years when the Grinnells moved into the park, a thirty-acre woodland tract between 155th and 158th streets, the Bloomingdale Road, and bordering the Hudson River.

John Jay Audubon's two sons, John and Victor, also lived in the park at the time. In his memoirs, George Bird noted that "Victor and John Woodhouse Audubon were still carrying on [their father's] studies and — probably — had just gotten out the great work, 'Viviparus Quadrupeds of North America.'" Both sons were also artists and their work was well displayed. John "was constantly receiving natural history specimens from correspondents all over North America, and painting the specimens he received."[3]

There were several families living in the park in the 1850s; most had a number of young children. Neither John Jay nor his sons had any business acumen and it fell to Lucy to try to keep the family solvent. She managed to build some rental houses and to sell some property, as well as teach reading and writing to the youngest park residents, who called her grandma. After her husband's death, she lived with her son Victor and held classes in her bedroom. It was here under her tutelage that Grinnell became particularly fascinated with Audubon's painting *The Eagle and the Lamb*, and they often talked about it. As she had promised, Lucy willed it to him when she died. Grinnell wrote in his memoirs that "she was a beautiful, white haired old lady with extraordinary poise and dignity; most kindly and patient and affectionate, but a strict disciplinarian and one of whom all the children stood in awe."

The Audubon houses were like nature museums, filled with artifacts, trophies from Audubon's western trips, mounted birds, and deer antlers on the walls supporting muzzle loaders, powder horns, and ball pouches. Paintings of birds and mammals filled the cluttered rooms, creating a visual setting for tales of Indians, big-game hunting, trappers and trading posts.

"And out in the barn," Grinnell wrote, "where we boys played were great stacks of the old red muslin-bound ornithological biographies and boxes of bird skins collected by the naturalist, and coming from we knew not where. John Woodhouse Audubon was in constant communication with various naturalists, and frequently received boxes of fresh

3. Grinnell Memoirs

specimens, around which, while they were being opened, the boys gathered to wonder at the strange animals that were revealed."[4]

Situated seven miles from the city, the park was a beautiful, rural parcel of land sloping down to the Hudson. Stands of huge oak, hemlock, and chestnut trees were havens for migratory birds in the fall; a large brackish pond jutting in from the Hudson enticed the children to go crabbing, fishing, swimming, and skating; dairy barns, stables, fruit orchards, and vegetable gardens completed the setting.

Growing up in the park was an adventure for the rambunctious children. They were seen swimming naked off the docks along the Hudson and were arrested; they stole chickens to roast on a fire; they smoked behind the barn, beat the pigs, and stole fruit from the neighbors' trees. One child was reported to have stolen a silver coin from a maidservant, but he also, reportedly, shared the candy. The Grinnell children were particularly high spirited and George Bird recalled that "the little boys of Audubon Park — all of them — ought to have been sent to some reform school." They were strictly disciplined, however, and neither snobbery nor bad manners was tolerated in this cultured environment in which self-discipline and family loyalty were expected.

Grinnell also remembered trips to his grandparents in Greenfield during his childhood, when his favorite pastime was examining his Uncle Tom's bird collection.

> Uncle Tom greatly impressed my youthful imagination by the stories he told of hunting and fishing adventures, and by the pictures he drew of birds. In his younger days he made a large collection of mounted birds and mammals which were in his father's house in Greenfield . . . In later years, and up until the time I was twelve or fifteen years of age, I had no plea-

4. Ibid.

> santer hours when at Greenfield, than those among Uncle Tom's birds in what was called the "bird room."[5]

Encouraged by his father, Grinnell began collecting birds to study, and from this early interest went on to become an expert taxidermist. He kept a workshop in his family's house for fifty years. It was this early exposure to his Uncle Tom's bird collection, along with his devotion to Lucy Audubon and his parents' enthusiastic support, that stimulated his interest and fascination in the natural world and strongly influenced his choice of his future career.

Grinnell's early education was spotty at best. Although he had never learned study skills, he made passing grades and reluctantly agreed to his father's wishes for him to attend Yale University. His freshmen year passed without incident, but by his sophomore year, ". . . I had become so much at home in New Haven and with my class, that I was perpetually in trouble. I was then barely seventeen years old, and quite without any sense of responsibility."[6] He got away with climbing a building of the college one night to splash his class year in red paint on the clock tower — but his luck did not last. Shortly afterwards, he was caught hazing a freshman and was suspended. With some other wayward students, he spent a year in Farmington, Connecticut, where they did little studying. After failing to pass his reentry exams, he was tutored again; finally he returned to college and graduated in 1870.

In the spring of 1870, he heard about a fossil-collecting expedition to the West, organized by Professor Othniel Marsh. "Having been brought up, so to speak, on the [travel] writings of Capt. Mayne Reid . . . between 1840 and 1850," Grinnell was determined to join the expedition, and

5. Ibid.
6. Ibid.

finally summoned the courage to ask Professor Marsh. Members of the group, most of whom went on to notable careers, included John R. Nicholson, later Chancellor of Delaware; James Wadsworth, New York Congressman; and Eli Whitney, inventor of the cotton gin.

Marsh had planned a five-month expedition through Nebraska, Wyoming, and Utah. General William Sherman offered his help to the paleontologist by arranging for Major Frank North of the U.S. Cavalry, two Pawnee scouts, and about fifteen cavalrymen to accompany the group through Indian territory.

The Marsh expedition was the first to be devoted entirely to collecting and studying remains of extinct toothed birds and dinosaurs and other fossils, as well as remains of living birds and mammals. Previous expeditions into the Midwest and West had been primarily for hunting, fishing, mining, exploring, military reconnaissance, and mapping. When Marsh's book on extinct toothed birds appeared in 1880, it included his observation that long-term survival of a species was the exception, not the rule. Charles Darwin wrote Marsh that in the twenty-year period since publication of *Origin of Species*, no one else had done as much to verify its basic conclusions.[7]

Upon his return to New York in the fall of 1870, Grinnell began working in his father's investment firm. But the trip west remained paramount in his thoughts, and in the summer of 1872, he was able to join Colonel Luther North (Frank North's brother, who also became a close friend) for the Pawnee summer buffalo hunt on the Great Plains in southern Nebraska.

Life on the prairie that summer where he felt at one with nature was exhilarating for the young scientist. Previously he had written many monographs and other scientific ar-

7. Reiger, *The Passing of the Great West*, p. 55.

ticles, and he now began writing for the general reader about the beauty of the area and his personal fascination with the Pawnee's way of life.

> The sun pushing aside the rosy curtains of the East commences to renew his daily life to all animated nature. He touches the more elevated bluffs with flaming light and suffuses the whole heavens with a ruddy glow. The leaves of the low willows, frosted with a coating of tiny dew drops, glisten in his light, and each silvery globule that hangs from the high grass reflects his image like a polished mirror. The waters of the Republican, dark and turbid . . . seem to become purer as they whirl along toward the Missouri. The mellow whistle of the meadowlark is heard from the prairie, the short cry of the migrating blackbird falls from on high, a flock of ducks on whistling wing pass over us on their way to those genial climes where frost and snow do not penetrate and where the rigors of winter are not felt.[8]

And in the evening when they returned to camp and the Pawnees are rejoicing over their bounty and enjoying the feast around the campfires, as darkness descends, the naturalist is once again moved by the scene before him:

> . . . the broad disk of the setting sun had rested on the tops of the western bluffs, and tipped their crests with fire. His horizontal beams lit up with a picturesque redness the dusky forms which moved about over the valley. Up the ravines and over the hills were stringing long lines of squaws, leading patient ponies, whose backs were piled high with dark, dripping meat, and with soft, shaggy skins. Late into the night the work continued and the loads kept coming into the camp. About the flickering fires in and before the lodges was feasting and merriment. Marrow bones were tossed among the red embers,

8. Grinnell,"Buffalo Hunt with the Pawnees," *Forest and Stream*, December 25, 1873.

> calf's head was baked in the hot earth, fat ribs were roasted, ka-wis boiled, and boudins eaten raw. With laughter and singing and story telling and dance, the night wore away.[9]

Despite this euphoria, in his reports he expressed concerns about the future. The buffalo, he noted, was vital for the Indian's way of life and every bit of the animal was used — the hides for warmth and shelter, the meat for food both in summer and winter. Sportsmen did not shoot enough animals to affect the herd, he felt, but it was the market gunners who were destroying the herds. While millions of buffalo still roamed the plain and the supply seemed inexhaustible, Grinnell had seen train after train rolling east, their boxcars filled with hides. The rest of the animal was left to rot on the plain, the bones later shipped to the East to be ground into fertilizer. Comparing the size of certain herds with figures recorded in Audubon's diary that Lucy had loaned him, he warned in an 1873 edition of *Forest and Stream* that "their days are numbered" and "unless some action is speedily taken, not only by the states, but by the National Government, these shaggy brown beasts . . . [will be] things of the past."

Although this was only his second trip west, it was the beginning of his lifelong interest in Native Americans and all areas of conservation. "His future career would reveal an ability for ceaseless work, great physical and intellectual discipline and a rare aptitude for exact observation . . . comprehending the need for a regional approach to this resource problem, through the agency of the federal government, he put himself in the forefront of conservation thought."[10]

Grinnell spent the rest of his active life visiting the Indians of the Plains. After extensive study of Grinnell's work,

9. George Bird Grinnell, *Pawnee Hero Stories and Folk Tales.*
10. Reiger, *The Passing of the Great West,* p. 29.

John Reiger wrote that he had the "rare ability to step inside the skin of the red man."[11] The respect and high regard in which Plains Indians held him is best illustrated by the names they gave him. The Pawnee called him "White Wolf," but after he was adopted into the tribe he was known as Pawnee Chief. The Cheyenne called him "Wikis," which meant bird, because of the way he came and went with the seasons; to the Gros Ventre he was "Gray Clothes" because of his dress on arrival from the East; and the Blackfeet named him "Fisher Hat," meaning that he had great power. His many books and articles reflected his understanding of Native American culture. He spoke several tribal dialects and also learned the universal sign language of the Indians.

In *The Golden Age of Anthropology*, Margaret Mead and Ruth Bunzel wrote, "Of . . . the books written about Indians, none comes closer to their everyday life than Grinnell's classic monograph on the Cheyenne. Reading it, one can smell the buffalo grass and the wood fires, [and] feel the heavy morning dew on the prairie." Another noted scholar, Mari Sandoz, observed, "Grinnell's work on the Cheyenne is the finest body of material on any American tribe."[12]

In New York in the fall of 1872, Grinnell's father decided to retire and let his son take over the investment firm. Within three months the country was plunged into the post-Civil War stock market crash, and the firm suffered severe losses. His father immediately returned to the firm and within a year was able to put it back on a sound basis. But Grinnell's dislike for the business was apparent; he finally convinced his father that he had to leave, and the company was dissolved. He went immediately to New Haven where he worked with Professor Marsh on various vertebrate paleontology projects, the first three years without pay.

11. Ibid., p. 2.
12. Ibid.

In 1873, Grinnell had begun contributing articles to *Forest and Stream* magazine. Publisher Charles Hallock was impressed with his work and asked him to be the natural history editor and book reviewer. His schedule of doing detailed, confining laboratory work at Yale and writing, combined with his trips west, became too heavy a burden. His health began to fail, and he was advised by his doctor to change his work "or be prepared to move into a lunatic asylum or the grave."[13] Reluctant to leave, he finally chose to change his work. In the spring of 1880, after receiving his Ph.D. from Yale, he moved back to New York where he became editor-in-chief of *Forest and Stream.* He later became its owner and publisher.

It was one of Grinnell's book reviews in the magazine that prompted an encounter with Theodore Roosevelt. Grinnell had been complimentary but also critical of Roosevelt's book "Hunting Trips of the Ranchman," questioning some of the author's observations, and the future governor of New York and president of the United States did not take it lightly. Having spent several years on his ranch after the deaths of his wife and mother, Roosevelt was annoyed that a reviewer should question the veracity of his account, and he stormed into Grinnell's office one morning in 1885 to demand an explanation. They in fact had a very amicable discussion because of their common interests and Grinnell's more extensive knowledge of the West. From then on, Roosevelt would take time to visit the Times Square office building to sit and discuss hunting, fishing, conservation, and "the broad country that [they] both loved."[14] Grinnell had spent more than a decade addressing these issues, and Roosevelt was impressed by his work and vision and de-

13. Grinnell Memoirs
14. John Mitchell, *Audubon Magazine,* March 1987.

pended on his judgment in the years ahead. Working together, the two men implemented some of the most important conservation legislation in the history of the country, which became the conservation cornerstone of Roosevelt's presidency.

Although their backgrounds were similar, they could not have had more different personalities: one, flamboyant, charismatic, ambitious; the other, slight, dignified, and self-effacing. Grinnell influenced Roosevelt's thinking, wrote some of his speeches, advised him on government appointments, and provided editorial advice on their coauthored books. They made an excellent combination, the budding politician and the pioneering scientist who understood the political system.

In an 1887 *Forest and Stream* editorial, Grinnell recommended that an organization be formed to provide leadership in securing conservation legislation at the state and federal levels. Roosevelt agreed to have a dinner party in New York and invite a group of wealthy gentlemen friends, all sportsmen, to hear the proposal for a series of regulations to curb sport-hunting excesses and abuses of wildlife, to protect the parklands, and to stress the importance of renewable resources in the forests. Renewable forest resources, as Grinnell noted, were already part of a European plan and ultimately were to become the foundation of modern wildlife management. The group of leaders in the effort took the name Boone and Crockett Club, and it became the country's first national conservation organization. John Muir's Sierra Club was established five years later. Grinnell continued to use *Forest and Stream* to promote conservation objectives. Most of the notable achievements of Roosevelt's administration were laid out in a series of books prepared by these leaders for the Boone and Crockett Club.

When Roosevelt became president, his friendship with

Grinnell continued. Despite Grinnell's sophistication, there was a naivete about him. In a letter to his niece after his first visit to the White House, he wrote:

> In Washington yesterday, I lunched with Mr. and Mrs. Roosevelt and had a very pleasant and amusing time. There were only three or four people there besides the family, but Mr. Roosevelt was very funny and I enjoyed myself. I was a little uncertain as I approached the house whether I ought to go down on my knees to him and kiss his hand when we met, instead of slapping him on the back and calling him old man, as has been my practice. But I found — as of course I really knew was the case — that he was quite the same as ever.
>
> Although I have been in Washington a great many times, this is the first occasion when I was ever within the White House grounds, and I felt quite a little curiosity about the inside of the executive mansion. It is not very impressive, for the two or three rooms which I saw were none of them as large as the library and dining rooms at the Hemlocks.[15]

All through his presidency, Roosevelt kept in contact with and depended on Grinnell, although he never publicly acknowledged his debt to Grinnell. "It was Grinnell who shaped Roosevelt's thinking and articulated the ideas that would later become the most enduring achievements of Roosevelt's administration . . . his tenure as President would see the implementation of the ideas he had absorbed from Grinnell."[16]

"I think of your Uncle George often," Frederick Walcott, former U.S. senator, conservationist, president of the American Wildlife Institute, Fish and Game commissioner, and author of the Duck Stamp Bill, wrote to Donald Page, Grinnell's nephew, in February of 1936. "All of the older men

15. Author's Collection
16. Paul Rundell, *Sports Afield Magazine*, December 1982.

inquired for him, or spoke of him with admiration and affection this week in Washington. I look upon him as the daddy of them all. He taught old TR the way in which to go, and he has been an inspiration and leader for all of us."[17]

With the time spent on his magazine, his books, and his voluminous correspondence; his trips west visiting Indians, parks, and virgin wilderness areas; and his efforts at lobbying Congress, Grinnell had to plan every moment to best advantage. His escape from such a rigorous schedule was to sit around a campfire, silently puffing his pipe while listening to and recording the Indians' stories. He also relaxed at "The Hemlocks" at Audubon Park, his home for fifty years. He was equally comfortable living in the two worlds of New York and the West.

Grinnell did not marry until he was fifty; although he remained childless, he loved children. He wrote a series of children's books and corresponded with his nieces and nephews and the children of friends when he was out West. They always awaited his return, curious and excited to hear his latest Indian stories. "Thank you so much for the lovely book you have sent me," young Teddy Roosevelt, Jr., wrote from the White House. "I have read it all. I got one of your books for Christmas, 'The Story of the Indian,' and I always carry my beloved 'Blackfoot Lodge Tales.' My brother and I have quite a managerie, 3 rabbits, 21 guinea pigs, 4 mice and 5 pigeons. I have a Manchester terrier besides. Your loving, Ted."[18] A great nephew recalled, "I remember, as a young boy, sitting at his feet, absolutely captivated by his Indian stories and western adventures."

With three generations living at Audubon Park, it was a closeknit family, and George Blake Grinnell doted on his eldest son. Writing to his brother in Greenfield, Massachu-

17. Author's Collection
18. Author's Collection

setts, in the 1880s, he noted, "George is on his way home now. I shall be thankful when he gets here. I am always anxious about his safety on these western journeys. Life would be worth very little without him. . . ."[19]

It was at "The Hemlocks" that Grinnell conceived the idea for the Audubon Society. For some time he had been appalled at the wholesale slaughter of song birds, game birds, and waterfowl for the millinery industry. He had seen as many as forty Baltimore Oriole skins lined up in a store window in New York, while another merchant spoke of selling 30,000 bird skins in one year to the fashion trade.

A first step was to prevail upon his sisters and their friends to refrain from buying or wearing any hats with feathers. And he began his crusade in *Forest and Stream* in 1886, announcing the formation of an association and soliciting subscribers with brochures. Within a year, a new magazine appeared, which he would call simply the *Audubon Magazine*, named as much for the artist as for his beloved Lucy.

The response by the public was instant and enthusiastic. Oliver Wendell Holmes heartily endorsed the plan, lamenting "the waste of these beautiful, happy, innocent and useful lives on which we depend for a large share of our natural enjoyment." The Reverend Henry Ward Beecher lent his support, as did John Greenleaf Whittier, who wrote, "I heartily approve of the proposed Audubon Society." Writer Charles Dudley Warner was more candid, advising Grinnell, "A dead bird does not help the appearance of an ugly woman."[20]

Within two years there were 50,000 subscribers to the magazine in thirty-nine states. By that point it had become too burdensome for him to continue, and Grinnell began

19. Ibid.
20. John Mitchell, *Audubon Magazine*, March 1987.

urging states to form their own organizations. In 1895, Massachusetts was the first to do so, while others soon followed.

For more than sixty years he spearheaded one campaign after another to protect the country's resources: parkland, mammals, birds, timberland, fish, and water sheds. It was in character, however, for the man himself to remain in the background: "Grinnell's gentlemanly desire to remain in the shadows . . . is one major reason why his true importance in the conservation movement has so long been obscured."[21]

> Grinnell is all but forgotten today, even among many of the organizations that he helped to found, and outside conservation circles his name is all but unknown. However, few men did more to launch the conservation movement and to set its sails. The reason for his present near-anonymity lies in the nature of the man himself. Grinnell was quiet, modest, and self-effacing to the point of shyness, but his personal accomplishments rival fiction. His circle of friends ranged from rough frontier trappers and Indian warrior to generals, millionaires, leaders in Congress, Cabinet members and presidents of the United States. . . . Once his self-woven cocoon of reserve was punctured, he was a stimulating conversationalist who could speak with authority on almost any subject. His letters, whether written to a brother Pawnee or to an officer of the Cabinet, sparkle with the sincerity, warmth and character of the man.[22]

Grinnell often wrote, "Of course I would rather keep in the background in this matter as far as the public is concerned."

In 1911 he decided to sell *Forest and Stream* and devote full time to writing, satisfied that the magazine had been a vital tool in the accomplishments made in all fields of con-

21. John Reiger, *American Sportsmen*, p. 251 n14.
22. James Trefethen, *Crusade for Wildlife*, p. 325.

servation. "A hundred years before the environment came into public consciousness, *Forest and Stream* called for the protection of watersheds and forests, complained about water pollution, supported the establishment of sound game laws and advocated the scientific management of our natural resources."[23]

Among Grinnell's many accomplishments were his efforts to enact legislation to protect the buffalo; riding into the Black Hills with General Custer in 1874 where, because of the discovery of gold that summer, he predicted the eventual bloody massacre; cofounding the Boone and Crockett Club; instigating a lobbying campaign that took twelve years to pass legislation to protect Yellowstone National Park from commercial interests; introducing Edward Curtis to his Indian friends and thus to the daily life and religious ceremonies of American Indians; recommending the creation of Glacier National Park; founding the Audubon Society; succeeding in getting legislation passed to forbid the commercial sale of game and to end the spring shooting of waterfowl; negotiating Indian territorial disputes at the request of two presidents; and recommending a policy to protect the nation's forest. Grinnell's work established an important successor in Aldo Leopold, who has been called the father of American conservation. "Grinnell's writings did much to mold the later interests and full career of Leopold," John Reiger noted.[24] Grinnell wrote countless articles on conservation themes, published thirty books, and belonged to all clubs and organizations devoted to these issues. He was among the founders of the American Game Protective Association from which evolved the present Wildlife Management Institute and the North American Wildlife Institute, the New York Zoological Society, the Society of American

23. Paul Rundell, *Sports Afield*, December 1982.
24. Reiger, *The Passing of the Great West*.

Foresters, and the National Parks Association and the National Park Educational Committee. And like many others in the forefront of America's conservation movement, he was an enthusiastic fisherman and hunter of big game, waterfowl and upland game birds.

Near the end of his life, confined to a wheelchair after a heart attack, he would gaze out the window of his townhouse on Fifteenth Street in New York City, watching the children play in the park below and reminiscing about his long career. Some of his most vivid recollections were of his second trip west for the Pawnee summer buffalo hunt:

> On the floor, on either side of my fireplace, lie two buffalo head skulls. They are white and weathered, the horns cracked and bleached by the snows and frosts and the rains and heats of many winters and summers. Often, late at night when the house is quiet, I sit before the fire and muse and dream of the old days; and as I gaze at these relics of the past they take life before my eyes. The matted brown hair again clothes the dry bone, and in the empty orbits the wild eyes gleam. . . . They dot the rolling hillsides, quietly feeding . . . or lie at ease on the slopes, chewing the cud and half asleep. . . . From behind a near hill, mounted men ride out and charge down toward the herd, until the black mass sweeping over the prairie numbers in the thousands.[25]

There had been heartbreak and disappointments through the years, but he was an optimist and wrote to a friend toward the end of his life, "I have had barrels of fun. In fact, I suspect, there is no one living who ever had so good a time during his life."[26]

When he died on April 12, 1938, in his eighty-ninth year, newspapers and magazines praised his lifelong crusade. The

25. Grinnell Memoirs
26. *Audubon Magazine*, March 1987.

New York Times referred to him as "the father of American conservation." A few days later, an editorial in the *New York Herald Tribune* concluded:

> Aside from Grinnell's prophetic vision, his forthrightness, his scholarship in the fields of zoology and Indian ethnography and the drive that empowered him to carry so many causes to successful conclusion, his outstanding personal characteristic was that of never failing dignity, which was doubtless parcel of the rest. To meet his eye, feel his iron handclasp or hear his calm and thrifty words—even when he was a man in his ninth decade—was to conclude that here was the noblest Roman of them all.

NOTE: I would like to thank Richard Burroughs for his helpful suggestions, as well as various members of my family who recalled interesting stories about Grinnell, both from his years at Audubon Park and later at his country place in Connecticut. I also thank Naomi Pascal, Editor-in-Chief, University of Washington Press, for her enthusiastic interest in the project; and my editor, Marilyn Trueblood, whose expertise was invaluable.

SOURCES

Diettert, Gerald A. *Grinnell's Glacier*, Mountain Press Publishing Co., 1992.

Goetzmann, William, and Kay Sloan. *Looking Far North: The Harriman Expedition to Alaska, 1899*, Princeton University Press, 1982.

Grant, Madison. *The American Review of Reviews*, June 1925.

Grinnell, George B. *The Harriman Alaska Expedition*, 1899. Privately printed.

——. Memoirs

——. *Pawnee Hero Stories and Folk Tales*, Forest and Stream Publishing Company, 1889.

Mead, Margaret, and Ruth Bunzel, eds. *The Golden Age of Anthropology*, George Braziller, 1960.

Mitchell, John. *Audubon Magazine,* March 1987.

Reiger, John ed. *The Passing of the Great West: Selected Papers of George Bird Grinnell,* Winchester Press, 1972.

——. *American Sportsmen and the Origins of Conservation*, Winchester Press, 1975.

Rundell, Paul. *Sports Afield,* December 1982.

Trefethen, James B. *Crusade for Wildlife,* The Stackpole Co., Boone and Crockett Club, 1961.

THE HARRIMAN EXPEDITION IN HISTORICAL PERSPECTIVE

by VICTORIA WYATT

Native Alaskans' experience with foreign encroachment started in southwestern Alaska in the mid-1700s with the settlement of Russian fur traders among the Aleuts, whom the Russians used as slave labor. In the last quarter of the eighteenth century, maritime explorers and fur traders from Spain, Britain, America, and France began frequenting the waters of southeast Alaska. Their contacts with the native peoples consisted primarily of trading for sea otter skins. The visitors brought new manufactured goods such as iron and wool; but while trade increased the material wealth of the native Alaskans, it also brought them alcohol and devastating diseases.

Russians advanced eastward in the late 1700s, establishing trading centers and Russian Orthodox missions as they went. One of their settlements, founded in 1799 near the site of present-day Sitka, became the headquarters of the Russian-American Company — the trading company that, by charter with the Tsar, had a virtual monopoly over Russian commercial affairs in Alaska.

The Russian-American Company experimented with a number of economic enterprises in the colony, including the exportation of ice, but only fur trading brought substantial financial rewards. In part because of the exploitation of the resource, these rewards dwindled by the middle of the nineteenth century, yet the cost of feeding and governing the colonies remained great. Faced with the need to defend her own borders, Russia could ill afford to maintain her American empire, and in 1867, Alaska was transferred to the United States. Since neither Russia nor the United States had signed treaties with native Alaskans, the land still belonged to native peoples and the United States became the new occupiers. American missionaries quickly started work among Alaskan native peoples, competing with the Russian Orthodox clergy who remained. American missionaries soon decried the effects of unscrupulous white people on native Alaskans.

In 1884, the United States formally made Alaska into a district with a civil government. Even before that, American entrepreneurs, often financed by companies in the lower states, began developing industries such as mining and salmon canning. Towns were founded in response to mining activities long before the Klondike gold rush. However, it was the discovery of gold along Canada's Klondike River in 1896 that brought Alaska to the forefront of America's attention. With the country in the midst of a depression, the promise of gold was a compelling draw to thousands of adventurers. Prospectors poured through southeast Alaska into the Klondike in 1897 and 1898. In 1898 gold was discovered near Nome. News of this strike reached Seattle in the summer of 1899, bringing a fresh flood of prospectors north.

Thus, in 1899 Alaska had reached a watershed. It had come to the forefront of the attention of the outside world. Its history had never been static — long before the arrival of Europeans, native peoples had traded with each other and exchanged ideas and customs as well as goods — but the changes brought by the Klondike and Nome gold rushes were especially rapid and far-reaching. The population of the region greatly increased in just a few years, and many native peoples previously isolated from foreign influence suddenly faced new challenges with the influx of nonnatives.

Edward H. Harriman's expedition in the summer of 1899 reached Alaska at this pivotal moment in its history. It contributed greatly to scientific knowledge of the region. Many of its results were published in eleven volumes from 1902 to 1905, and some of the expedition researchers continued to develop their findings long afterward.

The Harriman Expedition exemplified a type of interdisciplinary teamwork that seems revolutionary in the late twentieth century. The twenty-five specialists who traveled together on the *George W. Elder* represented branches of the natural sciences, social sciences, and fine arts—a miniature liberal arts conference. As the sponsor of the expedition, Harriman wanted the group to collect scientific data that would make groundbreaking contributions to geology, botany, ornithology, and cultural studies, but he also wanted to bring back his travelers' creative impressions of the landscape and peoples they met. He saw a vital place in the endeavor for poetry, art, photography—emotional and spiritual responses to the subjects under scientific scrutiny.

Thrown together for two months on a small ship, with no sustained contact with anyone else, the researchers traded perspectives on a daily basis. To ensure that such interaction was not left to chance, Harriman requested that members present and attend evening lectures in the ship's auditorium on topics ranging from technical biological research to analyses of current events in international affairs. The group had a mandate to enjoy their travels and their camaraderie, but they were also charged to work hard and to keep their focus on scholarly pursuits. Harriman expected to publish the results of the trip in a series of volumes devoted to various themes. At a time when some disciplines were still taking shape as formal branches of study, those scholars chosen for the expedition not only were at the top of their fields, but were shaping the future of their fields. The pressure on each to contribute to the achievements of the expedition must have seemed substantial.

George Bird Grinnell's research on the trip reflects this focus on scientific inquiry. His formal assignment was to report on Alaska's native peoples and on the fisheries; the resulting essays are included in this volume. His less formal role was to add his knowledge of Native Americans and cultural studies to the dynamic exchange of ideas aboard the *Elder*. At the time of the expedition, anthropology was beginning to emerge as a discipline. It scrutinized human cultures rather than zoological, botanical, and geological specimens, but its practitioners still aspired to the status of a science. They embraced aspects of the current scientific methodology, including close description and classification. Grinnell was familiar with the writings of Franz Boas, today often called the father of anthropology, who had published on native peoples of British Columbia. Grinnell referred to Boas's writing in his own "The Native Peoples of the Alaska Coast Region" (p. 152). He undoubtedly regarded Boas's detailed observation as the model to follow in his Alaskan studies.

Unlike Boas, Grinnell lacked the opportunity on the expedition for comprehensive studies of Alaskan native cultures. Staying for only a short time at each stopping place, he could neither observe closely nor work extensively with native consultants, two fundamental components of anthropological fieldwork. He shared this handicap with the natural scientists on board ship. Some of them broke away for short periods of time to camp in the wilderness and hunt animal specimens or study the local resources. Ultimately, however, their research was circumscribed by the expedition's schedule. Grinnell had to be content with a study that was part travel log.

He nevertheless did have opportunities for observation that surpassed those available to tourists on commercial steamships. Even in southeast Alaska, the region most heavily traveled by tourists, he enjoyed some unique excursions. A stop at the sealing camp in Yakutat Bay was off the beaten path of public transportation, as was a visit to the Tlingit village of Cape Fox. Both sidetrips occurred spontaneously; the group took full advantage of having a steamship at their disposal and changed their itinerary as research opportunities presented themselves. Grinnell's travels westward into the Aleutian and Pribilof islands took him to areas even less accessible to tourists. The islands were not, however, free from the influence of Americans. Prospectors were already moving into western Alaska, foreshadowing the gold rush in Nome, and Grinnell feared for the impact on native peoples.

In addition to a flexible itinerary, Grinnell enjoyed other advantages over most observers traveling in Alaska. Harriman's scientific vision for the expedition, as well as his position as an influential developer, opened doors for the group. In Sitka, the capital of Alaska, expedition members were hosted by Governor John Green Brady. He introduced them to Tlingit leaders there, as well as to Americans who could provide useful information. Grinnell spent time with Lieutenant George Thornton Emmons, who had studied Tlingit culture for years. Emmons arranged for the group to see ceremonial artworks that were still treasured and used by their native owners — spectacular masterpieces not usually shown to outsiders. Detailed sketches of some of these artworks appear in Grinnell's essay on the native peoples (pp. 137–83), reflecting the genre of contemporary scientific illustration.

Through such opportunities, Grinnell was able to record a remarkable amount of detail in the course of his travels.

Bombarded with impressions, he chose to devote his attention to native peoples' indigenous practices — what he called "their ancient customs and beliefs" (p. 138). The emerging discipline of anthropology endeavored, as much as possible, to study cultures as they were thought to exist before the influence of nonnative peoples. The rapid changes introduced by outsiders lent this mission a keen sense of urgency. Grinnell adopted this practice. Acknowledging that the Tlingits "are now greatly changed from what they were when the Russians first came to Alaska" (p. 138), he still concentrated on descriptions of traditional practices. He provided detailed accounts of hunting and fishing techniques, material culture, methods of handling canoes in the water, and manufacturing processes such as canoe-building. In his visit to Cape Fox, he paid careful attention to many details, describing the totem poles, architecture, burial grounds, and artwork found in the houses. He adopted the same focus in his discussion of Aleut and Eskimo peoples, emphasizing their diet, houses, sleeping arrangements, and physical features.

Since Grinnell lacked the opportunity to do comprehensive studies, the topics he addressed do not comprise a standard ethnography. Although he did record second-hand a brief description of a Tlingit potlatch, for the most part he wrote only on what he himself had seen during the expedition. He sought data about and wrote on indigenous cultural practices rather than cultural change. How native peoples had responded to nonnative influences — how they related to missionaries, a foreign education system, the introduction of a wage-labor economy, and a political system in which their rights were greatly restricted — was not central to his scientific inquiry.

He did focus on change in his description of the village of New Metlakatla on Annette Island in southeast Alaska (pp. 152–56). Here he made the point that the Tsimshian Indians living there under the control of missionary William Duncan had abandoned any customs that distinguished them culturally as native peoples. He wrote, "Except for their color, and for the peculiar gait . . . these people and their wives and children could hardly be told from any civilized community of a thousand souls anywhere in the country" (p. 153). Duncan's "model village" was well known at the time as an experiment of what could result from isolating native peoples from all other influences, not only from other native peoples but also from nonnative peoples. Duncan ruled in New Metlakatla as religious leader, political head, and judge. As time went on, the villagers—as well as white authorities in Alaska—became increasingly frustrated with the dictatorial powers he claimed. Nevertheless, Duncan's experiment remained the object of great interest and often admiration from nonnative commentators, as Grinnell's report suggests.

Grinnell had been impressed by William Duncan's program, which he said was "to change these Indians from the wild men that they were when he first met them, to the respectable and civilized people that they now are" (pp. 154–55). However, the influence of the miners in western Alaska disgusted Grinnell so much that he called it "the contaminating touch of the civilized" (p. 183). He concluded wistfully that "there is an inevitable conflict between civilization and savagery, and wherever the two touch each other, the weaker people must be destroyed" (p. 183). Grinnell's reference to "savagery" was not meant disrespectfully. In contrasting it to "civilization," he did not always equate the latter with progress.

When Grinnell turned his attention to native peoples living outside New Metlakatla, he focused on the opposite extreme: not the extent to which they had adopted nonnative customs, but the extent to which he could still observe "how they lived in their old-time way" (p. 156). From his published account, one would be unaware that several Tlingit leaders, all wearing formal attire, had attended the dinner that Governor Brady hosted for the expedition. Nor would one know that these leaders experimented with Harriman's Graphophone, enthusiastically recording songs and playing them back; nor that the following day, as the *Elder* steamed out of Sitka's harbor, the expedition was saluted by a Tlingit brass band playing rousing renditions of "Yankee Doodle" and other American patriotic songs.[1]

Such omissions from Grinnell's account simply underscore his mission to record information about old ways while such "data" were still available. Edward Curtis, the expedition photographer who later became famous for his photographs of Indians, formed a close friendship with Grinnell on the trip and adopted a similar approach to his work. He sought to preserve information about what he believed was a "vanishing race," and to that end he often omitted evidence of change from his photographs, even altering negatives to eliminate commercially manufactured goods. Recently his work has been criticized for such obfuscation. In a sense, though, he was doing visually what Grinnell and other anthropologists did on paper: focusing selectively on old ways rather than showing native peoples as they lived in the present.

Following the tradition of scientific writing, Grinnell maintained the voice of objective observer. In his essays, he did not discuss his own interactions with the Indians and Eskimos he met or speculate on their responses to meeting the Harriman Expedition, despite the fact that the travelers introduced native peoples to some new goods and ideas that interested them greatly — the Graphophone, for example, or the painstaking procedures of surveying. Like the biologists collecting specimens, Grinnell took it as his scientific

1. William H. Goetzman and Kay Sloan, *Looking Far North: The Harriman Expedition to Alaska, 1899* (New York: Viking Press, 1982), pp. 92–94.

mission to remain a detached observer of his data. With a few notable exceptions, he kept his personal opinions and his feelings about what he recorded to himself. In this he was very different from his colleague John Muir, whose writings reflect a spiritual relationship with the landscape he visited.

The larger impacts that the Expedition left in its wake were for the most part ignored in its record. Grinnell, for example, described Cape Fox village at length, giving detailed accounts of specific totem poles. He reported that there were nineteen standing in the village when they arrived, but he did not mention that there were considerably fewer standing when they left. Harriman had instructed the ship's crew to take down several of the poles and grave monuments to send to institutions in the United States. The California Academy of Science, the Field Museum in Chicago, the University of Michigan, the University of Washington, and the Peabody Museum at Harvard University, all received sculptures.[2] Expedition members also removed ceremonial artwork from the vacant houses. Although museums sometimes paid native owners, they justified such unlicensed collecting in the name of science.

To the Expedition participants, collecting artifacts was analogous to collecting animal specimens to bring back to scientific institutions for study. The impact was a bit different, however. With the removal of the artworks, the village that Grinnell so carefully described was altered. When his report was published, Cape Fox village no longer existed as portrayed in the text and illustrations. Furthermore, the artworks had not necessarily been abandoned. The Cape

2. Douglas Cole, *Captured Heritage: The Scramble for Northwest Coast Artifacts* (Seattle: University of Washington Press; Vancouver/Toronto: Douglas and McIntyre, 1985), p. 309. The discussion that follows here regarding the removal of the pole from Tongass is based on Cole's description (pp. 309–11).

Fox residents had left the village some six years earlier to move to the new town of Saxman. The fact that they no longer lived under the shadow of the poles, however, did not mean that they no longer claimed them or felt attached to them; such poles represented considerable expense and often honored relatives or ancestors. But removal of the Cape Fox poles was not an isolated incident. One month after Harriman's Expedition visited Cape Fox, members of the Seattle Chamber of Commerce took a totem pole from the Tlingit village of Tongass, believing it to be abandoned. In this case, the Tlingit family who owned the pole eventually received some compensation from the Chamber of Commerce, although the pole lived out its life in Seattle's Pioneer Square.

Since Grinnell usually assumed the role of the dispassionate observer, when he broke out of this mold, his own opinions assume special force. A poignant example is his discussion of the fate of the Eskimo peoples at Port Clarence. Here he described with sadness his predictions for the future, as the gold miners rushing toward Nome poured into the region. Grinnell wrote, "White men, uncontrolled and uncontrollable, already swarm over the Alaska coast, and are overwhelming the Eskimo." He reported that they were consorting with Eskimo women, selling liquor, and introducing devastating diseases. He predicted that "in a very short time they will ruin and disperse the wholesome, hearty, merry people whom we saw at Port Clarence and at Plover Bay" (p. 183).

Grinnell's concern for the preservation of the old ways also emerged in his study of the salmon industry (pp. 337–55). Much of this report, like his writing about native peoples, consists of detailed descriptions of fishing and canning operations. With these descriptions completed, however, he turned to a frank discussion of "greed" — destruction of resources at "so wholesale a rate that before long the canning industry must cease to be profitable" (p. 343). Referring to the industrialists, he dropped the voice of dispassionate observer and let his outrage show: "Thus the canners work in a most wasteful and thoughtlessly selfish way, grasping for everything that is within their reach and thinking nothing of the future. Their motto seems to be, 'If I do not take all I can get somebody else will get something'" (pp. 345–46).

Grinnell was not the first to expose such practices, and Congress had passed laws designed to regulate the canning industry. However, such laws were difficult and costly to enforce in rural Alaska. Grinnell reported flagrant violations that made him fear for the future of the resource. He also acknowledged the effects of the exploitation on native Alaskans. He pointed out that salmon streams were owned by native families, who relied on the salmon for food and never encroached on each other's streams. The canning industry had changed this: the rights of the native peoples to their streams had been usurped, their access to their own supplies had broken down, and now they were paid by canneries to fish indiscriminately.

Reporting such excesses, Grinnell emphasized that his concern was "not one of sentiment in any degree." Rather, the issue was one of economics. It consisted of a clear choice between rapid harvesting that destroyed the very source of profits, or the slower development of a sustainable resource that would yield a "perpetual" return. Presented in these terms, the choice seems an easy one to make — deceptively easy. The clash between a strategy of fast profit and one of sustainable development continues in Alaska and the Pacific Northwest today, as the last stands of old-growth forests face clearcutting. Until recently, southeast Alaska's Tongass National Forest, an important ecosystem admired by the Harriman Expedition, was being logged at a rapid rate even though the federal government had to subsidize the operations to make them profitable. Similar debates continue in

Oregon and Washington, where clearcutting threatens to bring about the extinction of endangered species.

The choice Grinnell posed between exploitation and sustainable development has long been a source of conflict in the history of Alaska and the Pacific Northwest. It undoubtedly will remain so for some time. Grinnell's observations serve as a vital reminder of all that is at stake. He was by no means against development. Traveling with the Harriman Expedition would have been a sore trial had he been. Rather, he advocated a reasoned approach, balancing short-term profit with preservation of the resources. Almost a century later, his discussion remains relevant.

Grinnell's concerns about depletion of the fisheries echoed those of some of his fellow travelers, who were shocked by the rapid destruction of fur seals. Their editorial comments suggest a role for scientific writing that extends beyond academia to influence public policy. Grinnell presented his reports to a scientific audience. At the same time, he undoubtedly hoped his observations about preservation would influence the legislators who set policy and the authorities who enforced it. In this he was not the first writer about Alaska to hope to have an effect upon the future of the region. Being so far removed from the seat of government in Washington, D. C., Alaska had an image as a frozen icebox that could contribute little to the nation's prosperity. In the late nineteenth century, some proponents of Alaskan development published books designed to dispel public ignorance and create more accurate perceptions of the region. As early as 1880, the Presbyterian missionary Sheldon Jackson described Alaska's geography, native cultures, natural resources, fisheries, and missions in *Alaska, and Missions on the North Pacific Coast*, concluding with a call for the establishment of civil government.[3]

3. Sheldon Jackson, *Alaska, and Missions on the North Pacific Coast* (New York: Dodd, Mead and Company, 1880).

One year prior to the Harriman Expedition, Alfred P. Swineford, a former governor of Alaska, published *Alaska: Its History, Climate and Natural Resources.* The book describes the geography and native peoples in detail, providing maps and photographs, some showing the glaciers visited the next year by the Harriman Expedition. In his conclusion, Swineford departed from his descriptive narrative with an emotional appeal for the political and economic future of Alaska. He declared that Alaska "is possessed of all the material elements essential to the growth of a great and powerful state." As the world began to measure productivity in natural resources rather than agriculture, he implied, Alaska stood to rise to the forefront of international commerce.

> With her wealth of precious metals, her great seams of coal, mountains of iron and veins of copper, her illimitable forests, wide area of grazing lands, fisheries from which the world's millions might be fed, to say nothing of the possibility, even probability, in the way of agricultural and horticultural development, who shall undertake to either definitely estimate or fix a limit to the value of Alaska's undeveloped resources?[4]

Other writers besides missionaries and government officials also promoted Alaska before the arrival of the Harriman Expedition. A thriving tourist industry had developed in southeast Alaska in the two decades prior to Harriman's trip, as mail steamships took tourists as far north as Glacier Bay. Some of these excursions were promoted by railroad companies that teamed up with steamship lines to offer packages to travelers from the eastern United States. Tourists enjoyed a railroad trip across the country and boarded the steamship in San Francisco, Portland, or Seattle. Some of them pub-

4. A. P. Swineford, *Alaska: Its History, Climate and Natural Resources* (Chicago and New York: Rand, McNally and Company, 1898), pp. 224–25.

lished travelogues, reporting on the scenery, the flora and fauna, and the native peoples they met. An early example, *Alaska: Its Southern Coast and the Sitkan Archipelago*, was written by Eliza Ruhamah Scidmore in 1885. While emphasizing the sublime, benign nature of the scenery, Scidmore identified strongly with wilderness explorers. She explained, "It is one of the easiest and most delightful trips to go up the coast by the inside passage and cruise through the archipelago; and in voyaging past the unbroken wilderness of the island shores, the tourist feels quite like an explorer penetrating unknown lands."[5] Her book combines personal observations with figures from the census, historical narrative, discussions of native culture, criticisms of federal education policy in Alaska, and accounts of federal funds paid for Alaska and returns already gained.

Another traveler inspired to write about her adventures was Septima M. Collis, the author of *A Woman's Trip to Alaska, Being an Account of a Voyage Through the Inland Seas of the Sitkan Archipelago in 1890*. She offered eloquent, poetic descriptions of the landscape and lavishly praised the activities of missionaries who gave her a tour of their work among the Tlingits of Sitka. Describing her thoughts as her ship steamed out of Sitka Harbor, she wrote:

> Yet I could not help thinking of the desolation to which our departure condemned those who had been so kind to us; nor of those poor souls whose darkness may never be dispelled by the enlightenment of education and civilization; and it occurred to me that if I owned the steamship line I would build a little hotel there, that the passengers might have an opportunity of occupying a week in excursions to points of interest, which it is impossible to reach in a large ship, and then life in Sitka would not be so intolerable; and that if I was the govern-

5. E. Ruhamah Scidmore, *Alaska: Its Southern Coast and the Sitkan Archipelago* (Boston: D. Lothrop and Company, 1885), p. 3.

> ment of the United States, I would put the Indians under such discipline that their quarters should be subject to inspection, and their children compelled to go to school. What two great boons these would be to Sitka and how easy to accomplish both.

She concluded, "But the scenery is so beautifully grand that I must keep my moralizing for some future time."[6]

By the summer that Grinnell and his Harriman Expedition colleagues visited Alaska, then, much had already been written in America about the region—and, implicitly or explicitly, much of what had been written addressed its resources and prospects for development. The scientists understood that they were exploring areas already known to a large public. If they had not grasped this on embarking, it became graphically clear in Glacier Bay when they came across wooden boardwalks along the moraine of Muir Glacier. These boardwalks helped tourists walk on the moraine. Muir must have been startled that the glacier he had explored in 1879 had become a tourist attraction in twenty short years.[7] Grinnell observed other effects of a tourist industry when he commented on the Tlingit women in Juneau "sitting on the wharves offering their baskets and other simple articles made for trade" (p. 156).

The Harriman Expedition reports added to the information about a region that was increasingly of interest to a general public as well as to the scholarly community. While they wrote primarily for scientific colleagues, Harriman's researchers were aware that their reports could influence the future development of the region. Harriman himself, eyeing the possibility of a transportation network under the Bering

6. Septima M. Collis, *A Woman's Trip to Alaska, Being an Account of a Voyage Through the Inland Seas of the Sitkan Archipelago in 1890* (New York: Cassell Publishing Company, 1890), p. 127.

7. Goetzman and Sloan, pp. 71–72.

Sea, appreciated the link between science and industry. Thus, when the Expedition reports were published, they potentially held value for a range of readers: scientists, developers, even armchair travelers.

Grinnell's essays appeal to a similarly broad audience today, if a different one. They are important as primary sources documenting the emergence of anthropology as a discipline. The Expedition's emphasis on science underscores the scientific aspirations of early cultural scholars, and Grinnell's writing exemplifies the tone and approach of their studies. His reports provide useful information in penetrating detail from a keen observer.

The reports also hold interest because they reflect Grinnell's own philosophies. On the one hand, they demonstrate his interest in scientific tone and empirical observation. On the other hand, they show that he found a place for editorializing. Never wanting to devolve into "sentiment," he still recognized the relationship between scientific knowledge and economic policy. He felt recommendations about the latter were definitely in order. Not inconsequentially, his research was made possible by a grant from private industry, foreshadowing contemporary relationships between private industry and scientific inquiry.

In addition, Grinnell's reports give evidence of an era when researchers became involved in a number of pursuits and gained legitimacy in more than one field. Harriman included Grinnell on the expedition because of his earlier studies of native cultures, but Grinnell is best known today for his energetic work helping to found conservation groups, most notably the National Audubon Society. His philosophies highlight the complexity of the conservation movement then and now. Without opposing development, he advocated a rational approach to it with an eye toward preservation and sustainable profits. Scientific scrutiny was his goal in the Harriman reports, but he infused his writing with the message that development is not necessarily synonymous with progress.

The interdisciplinary impetus of the Harriman Expedition offers much of value today. Contemporary academic pursuits tend to be highly specialized and compartmentalized. Perhaps the closest analogy currently to Harriman's meeting of disciplines can be found in commission work, where interdisciplinary teams study research policies and make recommendations to agencies such as the National Park Service and the National Forest Service. Such efforts lack the intensive encounters involved in a two-month steamship expedition. Further, such broad-based commissions generally focus on problem-solving rather than on basic research. Specialization has some obvious benefits, but it also comes at a cost. Disciplinary boundaries are artificial constructs that do not reflect reality well. Much is lost when such boundaries interfere with the exchange of ideas.

Fortunately, today there is increasing recognition of the value of interdisciplinary work—a value inherent in the Harriman Expedition almost a hundred years ago. Recently biologists have applied ecosystem models to resource management, emphasizing the relationships between species instead of treating each species as an autonomous entity. The ecosystem model focuses on very real processes and relationships rather than on artificial boundaries. Most often applied to landscapes, the model also has application for human knowledge. No line of inquiry exists in a vacuum: the sciences, social sciences, and humanities are all influenced and informed by social values and human creativity.

The vision that brought the Expedition to Alaska in 1899 embraced the forest as well as the trees. The experiences shared by those traveling on the *Elder*, the relationships they formed and the exchange of ideas they enjoyed exemplified interdisciplinary cooperation. George Bird Grinnell made a lasting contribution to the Expedition's quest for knowledge. His essays add life and human interest to the record of 1899 Alaska; they also lend insight into the philosophies informing the history of conservation movements in the United States. Throughout his life, Grinnell remained focused on relationships between several disciplines and the contributions they together make to preserving sustainable resources for human communities. This vision holds much relevance today.

UNIVERSITY OF VICTORIA, CANADA

ESSAYS FROM THE HARRIMAN EXPEDITION

PHOTOGRAPH BY CURTIS

ELSON, BOSTON

DESERTED INDIAN VILLAGE, CAPE FOX, ALASKA

THE NATIVES OF THE ALASKA COAST REGION

BY GEORGE BIRD GRINNELL

THE COASTWISE INDIANS

HALIBUT HOOK.

ALL along the southeastern coast of Alaska, from Port Tongass to Kachemak Bay, are scattered the villages of the Alaska Indians. They are a hardy race. Living on the shore, bold mariners and sea hunters, they are also mountaineers, familiar with the towering peaks, the dreadful cliffs, and the mighty glaciers of the iron-bound coast. In their frail canoes they venture far to sea in pursuit of the fur-seal, the sea-otter, and the whale; or thread their perilous ways amongcrowdingice-bergs to capture the hair seal. In spring, when the coat of the white goat is long and shaggy, they clamber skyward, first through the forests, and then over the broken rocks, until they reach his feeding ground,

NATIVE WOMEN AND CHILDREN, ALERT BAY, BRITISH COLUMBIA.

and there kill him for his flesh, and for his fleece, which they weave into blankets. High up among the rocks, too, they trap the marmots and ground squirrels whose skins sewn together serve them for robes.

The changing seasons give them their seal, their salmon, and their berries; their fish, their fowl, and their deer—the latter driven down from the high mountains by the deep snows of winter, or in summer forced by the flies out of the forests to feed along the beach. They fish, they hunt, they feast, they dance; and, until the white man came and changed all their life, they lived well.

TLINKIT WAND, USED IN DANCING.

Although belonging to three different linguistic families, Koluschan, Skittagetan, and Chimmesyan, their environment is essentially the same, and this means that their ways of life do not markedly differ. Although they are now greatly changed from what they were when the Russians first came to Alaska, they still preserve not a few of their ancient customs and beliefs.

Unlike the Indian tribes of our Western States, most of which have treaties with the government by which they are supported wholly or in part, these dwellers along the Alaska coast depend for their subsistence wholly on their own exertions and draw their food largely from the sea. They are essentially a race of fishermen. Their main dependence is the salmon, of which enormous numbers are caught, but they also secure an abundance of halibut, and, at certain seasons of the year, of other fish. The introduction of the products of civilization has done away with the use of the old-time fish-line, which was made of knotted lengths of the stem of the giant kelp, but they still use hooks of primitive form, though now the unwieldy implements are tipped with iron, instead of with bone as in ancient days. Not only do they procure their animal food largely from the sea, but it yields them as well two or three sorts of seaweed, one of which is eaten fresh, while another is dried, pressed into cakes, and used as an ingredient of soups and stews.

TLINKIT DANCE RATTLE.

The salmon are captured in a variety of ways; by means of spears and gaffs, but also very largely in traps. These commonly consist of a barrier extending across the stream, but with an opening through which the salmon can pass. Above the opening is a trap from which the fish cannot escape. Sometimes merely a close barrier is built. The instinct of the salmon, when seeking their spawning beds, teaches them to always push onward toward the head of the stream; they never turn back. And if a barrier is built which prevents their working their way up against the current, they will remain below it, always trying to force their way through, until they die. When captured in large numbers, the salmon are dressed and hung on the poles of the drying scaffold, exposed to sun and wind, until at last they are dry enough

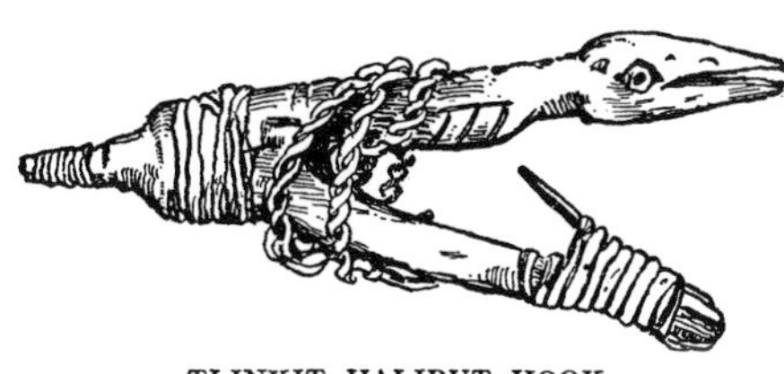

TLINKIT HALIBUT HOOK.

to be packed away. In this condition they will keep indefinitely.

Besides the fish that they catch, the Indians do much hunting in the mountains and on the islands along the coast. Deer are abundant, and great numbers of them are killed at all seasons of the year. In winter, the native steals along in his canoe, close to the shore, looking for deer that have ventured out of the forest to feed on the seaweed and the grass along the beach. Very quietly he slips up to the game, and when near enough, kills it by a shot from his rifle. Many of the men are good hunters and do not fear to attack the great brown Sitka bear, which is larger than the grizzly and quite as much disposed to fight.

TLINKIT CANOE, SOUTHEAST ALASKA.

On the Alaska coast the water is the common highway. Away from the settlements there are no roads nor trails, for the many wide inlets and rivers which run back into the mountains at frequent intervals prevent land travel up and down the coast. The Indians make all their journeys by canoes, and in the handling of these they are most expert. A child is scarcely out of its cradle before a tiny paddle is thrust into its fist. Infants not more than three or four years old may be seen paddling for hours at a stretch. Thus trained from childhood, these Indians are enormously strong in their arms and hands, and can accomplish a wonderful amount of work of this kind without showing fatigue. The upper part of the body is much more robust than in the Indians of the Plains.

Different types of canoes are in use in different localities. All the sea travel is done by means of paddles, but in ascending rivers where the current is too swift to be overcome by paddling, poles are used. An Indian, as he drives his canoe upstream against the turbulent current, keeps close to the bank and takes advantage of all the eddies, pushing along quietly until he has almost reached the swiftest water; then fixing his pole firmly against the bottom he leans back against it and sends the light shell darting upstream. Before its way has ceased he has again secured a good hold on the bottom, and no matter how furious the rapid, the little craft, held perfectly straight, moves steadily forward until the quiet water above has been reached, and the pole is laid aside for the paddle.

HUNYA SEAL HUNTERS, GLACIER BAY.

These canoes are always made from a single piece of timber. In southern Alaska and British Columbia where the white cedar grows, this is the favorite wood, and from its trunks canoes are hollowed out which are sometimes eighty feet in length. Such were the great war canoes in which the fierce Haida and other peoples of the north used to make their war journeys to harry their enemies to the southward, to plunder their villages, and to make captive their people, whom they brought away to their island home as slaves. These great war canoes were very wide and so deep that a man standing in the bottom of one could not see over its sides.

In making the canoe, the log is first roughly shaped and hollowed out by fire, water or moist earth being used to control the burning. After this has progressed as far as is safe, a chisel formed of a piece of steel fixed in a wooden handle, is used to chip off the wood in little flakes, both from the outside and inside until the shell is reduced to the proper thickness.

After the canoe is shaped, the gunwales are slightly sprung apart, by wetting with water brought almost to

CARVING OF TLINKIT CANOE.

the boiling point by means of heated stones, so as to give greater flare to the sides, and in the larger canoes are held in position by braces or narrow strips of timber stretching across the boat, and sewed or lashed to the gunwales by cedar twigs made flexible by steaming. Smaller canoes need no such braces. The Indians have no models and the eye is the only guide in making the canoe, but the lines are always correct and always graceful.

Paddles are variously made of spruce, hemlock, and sometimes of maple brought from the south. They are from four to five feet long, and vary in shape of blade and handle with the different tribes. Some have a cross piece for a handle ; others are straight. Usually the blade is about four inches wide and terminates in a long, sharp point. Sometimes the blades are ornamented with carvings.

The canoes are never left in the water. When brought to shore the occupant steps out on the beach and lifts or drags the canoe up above high-water mark. This must be done, for a very little battering by the sea, or a knock or two on the beach, might split and ruin the boat. When on the beach, exposed to the air and sun, it is always covered by cloths or skins which are kept wet, for if the wood of the canoe should become dry and heated it would warp and crack.

The canoes used by the Indians of Koluschan stock are not commonly carved as are those of the Indians of northern British Columbia, but this is not because these Indians are not skillful carvers. In the totem poles and in the ornamentation of their houses and of many of their implements and utensils we have good evidence of the high artistic talent of these Indians. They are expert weavers, and make blankets from yarn that is twisted from the fleece of the white goat. They also make mats of great beauty, hats from the inner bark of the cedar, and baskets from cedar bark or from roots, which are absolutely water tight. In ancient times they cooked their

TLINKIT BOX, CARVED AND PAINTED.

TLINKIT BASKETS.

food in such baskets, boiling the meat or fish in the water which they held, made hot by the introduction of red-hot stones. Ropes and lines are twisted from the bark of the cedar and are still used for many purposes. Their baskets, oil boxes, ceremonial blankets and clothing are, as is well known, beautifully ornamented, and they carve elaborately in wood and stone.

Like other Indians more to the southward, those in Alaska are great respecters of wealth. The rank of any family depends rather on the accumulation of riches and the subsequent giving them away by its head, than on bravery or success in war or in hunting. The highest ambition of these Indians is to acquire property in order that they may give it away again, and wealth so evidenced seems to form among them the standard of rank. He who gives away most is the greatest chief, and at subsequent 'potlatches,' or occasions for presenting gifts, he receives a present proportionate to the amount of his own gift. Therefore, when an Indian has accumulated more or less money or other property, he is likely to purchase great quantities of food, calico, and blankets, and then to invite all his friends up and down the coast to a potlatch. In old times, the feast consisted of boiled deer meat and salmon, with unlimited crackers, tea, sugar, and molasses. Each guest has all the food he can eat, and each one is given so many yards of calico. The important visitors receive blankets, and part of the blankets are tossed from the housetop into a crowd of young men,

TLINKIT CARVING REPRESENTING BEAVER.

PART OF HOUSE FRAME, ALERT BAY, BRITISH COLUMBIA.

and scrambled for by them. The festal occasion may last for several days or a week, and when it is at an end the Indians go their several ways, leaving the giver of the potlatch a poor man. When the next one takes place, however, he recovers a portion of his wealth, and after a few more he is better off than ever — for the time being. Canoes may be given away at these feasts, or guns and ammunition, and the greater the gift the more is due the giver, when those who have been his guests themselves give potlatches.

DESERTED VILLAGE, CAPE FOX.

The villages occupied by these Indians are permanent. The houses are made of rough planks, split or hewn from large trees — to the southward the cedar and to the northward the spruce — and roofed with shingles split from the trees, though in olden times the roofs were more commonly of planks similar to those used in the construction of the walls. These houses, which are often forty feet square, and sometimes even larger, were usually without floors in old times, though the bed places which run around the walls were raised a foot or two from the ground, and were formed of planks hewn smooth by a slow process of chipping, which must have been very laborious. Often gravel is brought into the house, and the floor covered with it, so that even in wet weather it does not become muddy. The fire is built on the ground in the middle of the room, and the smoke escapes through narrow openings in the roof, for usually the planks do not quite meet at the ridgepole, so that the sky may easily be seen. Such houses are occupied by a number of families, usually related in some degree.

Such a village may consist of ten, fifteen, or twenty large houses placed side by side on the bank just above the beach, and not more than two or three feet above high-water mark. The striking feature of the village is the totem poles, some of which are fifty or sixty feet high, erected by chiefs or principal men in front of their houses. They are elaborately carved with figures of men, frogs, birds, and various mammals. Some of them indicate the descent of the man who erected them; others are burial trees in which are deposited the ashes of the dead. Not infrequently more than one totem pole is erected before a house, and in a deserted village which the Harriman expedition visited there were nineteen poles, while the houses numbered only fourteen. The illustrations give a very clear idea of the character of these poles. One represented a succession of bears, one above the other, while the pole was sur-

TOTEM POLES, CAPE FOX.

PHOTOGRAPH BY CURTIS — JOHN ANDREW & SON

Beaver Totem, Deserted Village

mounted by the carved figure of an eagle; this was the tallest pole in the village. Another, which from its appearance seemed to have been standing for very many years — for it was gray with weather, and long strings of lichen hung down from it — consisted of the stout upright twenty feet in height, surmounted by an almost equally stout cross pole, on either end of which sat a large carved toad. One much taller than this was surmounted by a beaver holding a stick across his jaws. Another, not very tall, had near the top a large hole from which a bear's head and shoulders protruded. Representations of the tracks of the bear were painted on the pole from the ground up to the hole from which he looked. The topmost figure on most of these totem poles was a bird, presumably an eagle, but in one or two cases this figure was a man wearing a conical hat. The frog, the bear, the eagle, and the killer whale were frequently represented on the posts, and on one very large pole were carved the figures of three enormous halibut, one above the other.

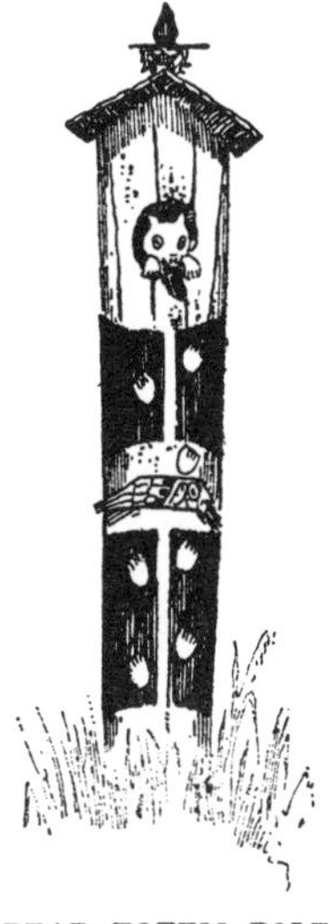

BEAR TOTEM POLE, CAPE FOX.

TOTEM POLE, ALERT BAY.

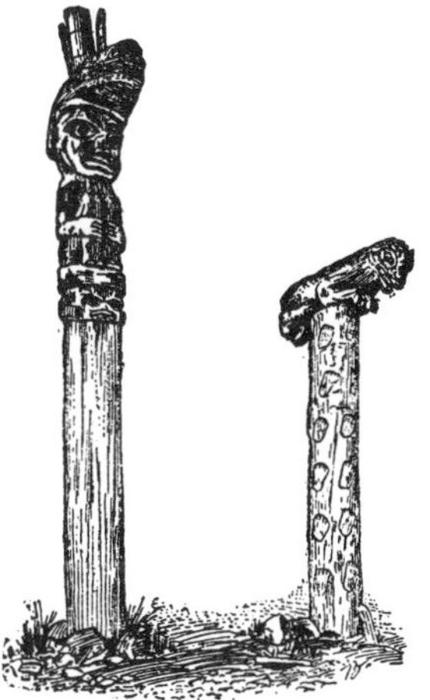

TOTEM POLES, WRANGELL.

In this village the front of the principal house was highly ornamented by painting. The decoration represented a conventionalized bear

EAGLE

BEAR

INSIDE OR ROOF-POST TOTEM POLES, CAPE FOX.

TOTEM POLE, WRANGELL.

split from the tail to the nose along the middle line, and the two halves painted one on either side of the front of the house, so that the two halves of the nose met above the door. The ear on either side protruded above the sloping roof line.

The ornamentation is by no means confined to the exteriors of the houses. In some cases the roof posts, or uprights supporting the enormous rafters which uphold the roof on either side of the house are highly carved and painted, and at times other carvings, usually also painted, are set up in different parts of the building. Most of the totem poles seen by tourists visiting Alaska are at Wrangell. Several of these are shown in the accompanying illustrations. In the houses

PHOTOGRAPH BY CURTIS — JOHN ANDREW & SON

CHIEF'S HOUSE, DESERTED VILLAGE, CAPE FOX

are kept the elaborately carved and painted masks used in ceremonial and religious dances, and highly reverenced for the mysterious power they are supposed to possess. They are of diverse forms and patterns: some represent the heads of birds and beasts; others the human face in repose or distorted.

The variety in these masks is quite extraordinary. They are an important feature of all the ceremonial dances practiced by these Indians, and as these ceremonies occupy a considerable portion of the people's lives, it may be imagined that the masks are numerous and diverse. Besides the forms mentioned, masks often represent conventionalized animals hardly to be recognized

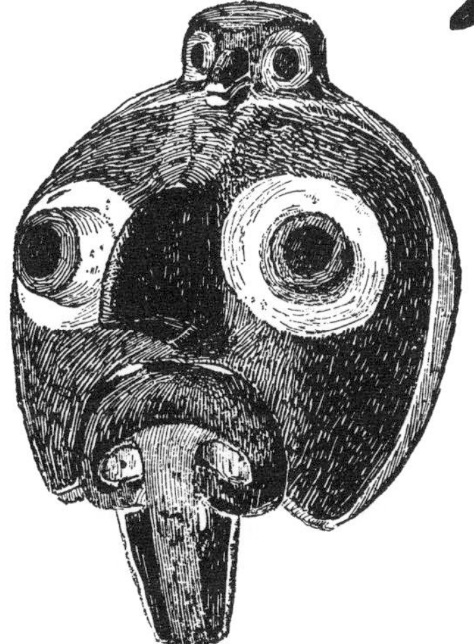

TLINKIT MASKS.

except by one who has made the subject a study, while still others represent mythical and sacred personages. Certain rayed masks, not unlike the one shown on page 149, are regarded as sun masks. Masks are often ornamented with fringes of hair, down, cedar bark, or quills; others are inlaid with pieces of abalone shell or bits of ivory. Those representing the heads of huge birds are sometimes so arranged that by pulling certain strings the bills may be rapidly opened and shut so as to make a clattering sound. Masks of another class are double. The outer portion is divided vertically — and sometimes horizontally — in two or four pieces, which are hinged to the solid inner piece. These outer pieces, when strings are pulled, fly apart and outward and reveal another face within. Of the two faces the outer one may be that of an animal and the inner of a man.

INDIAN GRAVE AT WRANGELL.

The most common form of animal mask represents the eagle, raven, puffin, hawk, bear, wolf, or deer. To the left on page 149 is a puffin mask.

At a little distance from the village, usually overlooking the water, sometimes on a steep side hill, or on a little point which forms the side of a bay, are the graves of some of the dead. Common people are usually burned and their ashes put away, either in a hole bored in one of the totem poles, which is afterwards plugged up, or in a little box on a pole in the common burial ground, or in a dead house as shown in the sketch on p. 152, but the shamans, or mystery men, are not burned. They are buried with ceremony, on or under the ground, and over them is often erected a platform which supports one or more images, sometimes of colossal size. On such a grave in the village above referred to were the carved wooden figures of two bears, perhaps six or seven feet tall, sitting on their haunches. Over another was a more ancient image, a huge bird built of wood, with outstretched wings

GRAVES OF SHAMANS, CAPE FOX, ALASKA.

and a long beak. In a general way it resembled a heron flying, and reminds one strongly of the mythical bird

HoXhoq spoken of by Dr. Boas in his account of the social organization of the Kwakiutl.

At Taku Harbor we visited the deserted remains of a small Indian village near which were several dead houses. These were examined by Dr. Merriam who found in them charred human bones and teeth. After the bodies had been burned the bones had been gathered up and put into wooden boxes, or in some cases simply laid on pieces of board and placed inside the dead houses.

INDIAN DEAD HOUSES CONTAINING CHARRED HUMAN BONES, TAKU HARBOR.

In striking contrast to this village and to the Tlinkit camps seen farther to the northward, was the spectacle witnessed during our call at the colony of New Metlakahtla, on Annette Island. It was to this barren island that Mr. William Duncan, in 1887, brought his little flock of civilized Metlakahtla Indians, when the combined persecutions of Church and State had made British Columbia too hot to hold them. Abandoning all the property they had accumulated in the town that they had made, they pushed their way across the straits to this island in the

United States, and like any colony of settlers in a new country, began to fell the timber to build themselves houses, to erect a sawmill, and to cultivate the ground.

TOWN HALL AND CHURCH, NEW METLAKAHTLA.

Only a few years had passed when the property of the colony was as great as it had ever been, and since that time it has gone on prospering. The town is laid out with straight, broad streets, and wide board sidewalks. Each house and its garden is surrounded by a fence; the people wear civilized clothing, work at the fishing, in the sawmill, or in the cannery for six days in the week, and rest on the seventh, attending church service in the edifice which they erected with their own hands, and which is a piece of architecture which would be called beautiful in any land. Except for their color, and for the peculiar gait, which seems to be common to all these fishing Indians, these people and their wives and children could hardly be told from any civilized community of a thousand souls anywhere in the country.

It took many years for Mr. Duncan to change these Indians from the wild men that they were when he first met them, to the respectable and civilized people that they now are. Whatever they are to-day Mr. Duncan has made them, and he himself and no other is responsible for the change in the individuals that have been born and lived and died, and still live in this colony during the period of his wise and beneficent influence over them. He has kept them by themselves, teaching them to live as the white man lives, and yet not letting the white man come in among them. They govern themselves in town-meeting fashion, consulting Mr. Duncan frequently as to what they ought to do. Liquor is unknown among them, except when occasionally some of the young men go off to a distance to visit other villages, or to work in other canneries, and while absent drink and get into trouble. Then they return to Metlakahtla and receive good advice, and are strengthened anew to resist temptation.

Within the past two or three years, since the discovery of gold in Alaska, persistent efforts have been made to induce Congress to deprive these Indians of the home they have made for themselves on Annette Island; it has been proposed to confine the Indians to a small portion of the island, and to throw the remainder open to settlement. The ostensible reason advanced for such a course is that deposits of precious metal have been found on the island, and ought to be worked. As a matter of fact, this is not true. The island has never been prospected at all, for the reason that whenever white men land Mr. Duncan's police promptly arrest and expel them. This is done in accordance with the agreement made with the colony by the United States Government, which, before they moved to Annette Island, promised that if they would take it for their home they should never be disturbed. This promise should be kept. To open a part of this island to settlement, as proposed, would be to deprive the Indians of their means of subsistence, for it would take away from them the water power which runs their sawmill, and the salmon on which they depend for support. Such a wrong should not be permitted.

The Harriman expedition first saw Alaska Indians at this village of New Metlakahtla. We landed here on

NEW METLAKAHTLA.

Sunday morning, early in June, and were most kindly received by Mr. Duncan, who showed us about through the public buildings, talked entertainingly of his experience with these Indians, and later preached in Tsimpsian a sermon to a large congregation of Indians.

The village, as we wandered through it that Sunday morning, was like an old-fashioned New England hamlet in its peaceful quiet. There was no one abroad. Until the church bell began to ring the people remained in their houses, and then from each door a little family stepped out, and all took their way toward the church until the broad board walks near the edifice were crowded with the people. It would be hard to imagine a more decorous and attentive audience; obviously their thoughts were fixed on the discourse to which they were listening, and neither man, woman, nor child turned eyes toward the company of strange white people which crowded into the church behind them.

Their sawmill, salmon cannery, and four stores give the community a comfortable support. Among the men are blacksmiths, carpenters, shoemakers, tailors, and other handicraftsmen. They have built their own houses, their church, their school-house, guest-house, and council-house. Some of the dwellings are two stories and a half in height, comfortable in appearance, and neatly kept.

CARVED DANCING MASK.

At Juneau a few Indians were seen, chiefly men in their canoes starting out for the fishing, or women sitting on the wharves offering their baskets and other simple articles made for trade. At Sitka, however, the Indians were more numerous. Here we had an opportunity not only to see something of the Indians and of how they lived in their old-time way, but also to examine the Sheldon Jackson Museum, and in some of the stores, a great deal of material in the way of the primitive implements which are now practically discarded.

When the Russians reached the place where Sitka now stands they found a camp of

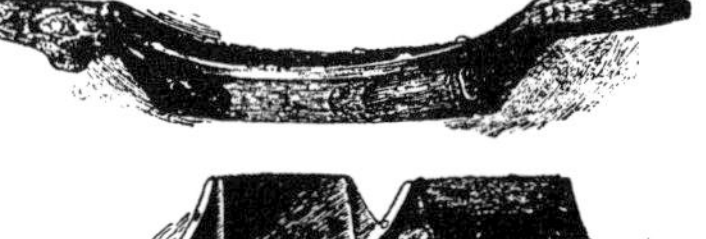

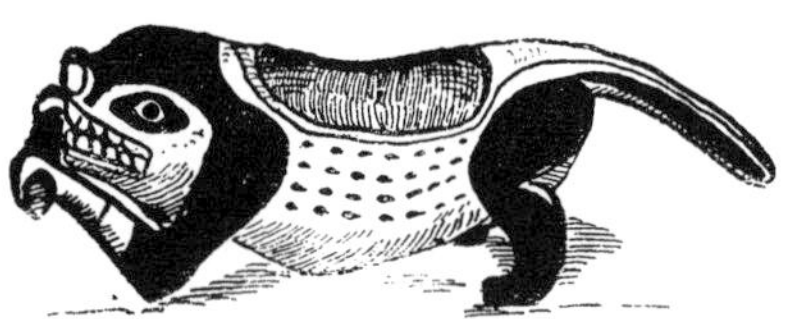

CARVED DISHES, SITKA.

Indians from a village called Sitko, on the opposite side of the island. The Russians questioned the Indians as to who they were, what was the name of the place, and on other matters; but as the Russians could speak no Tlinkit, and the

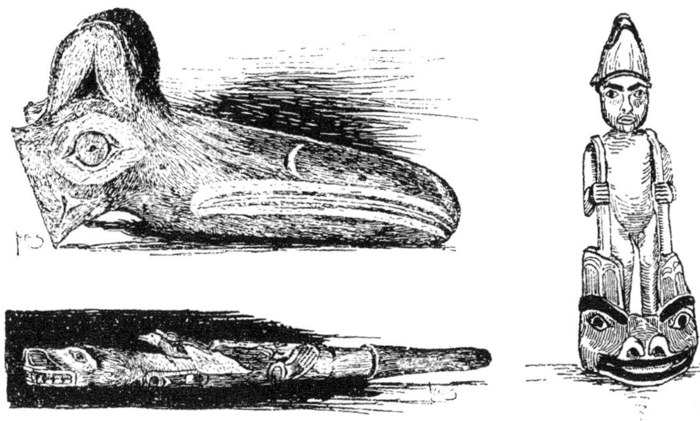

TLINKIT CARVINGS.

Indians no Russian, they did not very well understand each other. The Indians told the Russians that they were the Sitko, the people from that village; but the Russians understood them to mean that this was the name of the place where they were camped, and so they called it Sitka, and Sitka it has been ever since, although the real Sitko is far away.

At Sitka as everywhere on the coast, the houses of the Indians are built close above the beach. In exterior appearance they do not differ from those of the white man, but usually there is only a single room within on the ground floor. Occasionally a house front is ornamented with elaborate paintings, in the old style.

PAINTING ON FRONT OF HOUSE OF CHIEF ANNAHOOTS, SITKA.

The Indians still observe many of their old customs and possess not a few of their ancient ceremonial and religious dresses, though neither the customs nor the dresses are often seen by the whites. Through the great kindness of Lieutenant Emmons of the Navy, we were enabled to visit one or two of the principal men, and see objects, such as elaborate dancing masks, shaman's hats, Chilkat blankets, and other things rarely exposed to the common eye.

TLINKIT SHAMAN'S HEADDRESS.

While at Sitka we learned that many of the Indians were absent at Yakutat Bay, where they were catching the hair seals, whose oil throughout the year furnishes an important part of their subsistence.

TLINKIT SHAMAN'S HAT.

On reaching Yakutat Bay we found three camps of Indians all engaged in the hair seal fishery. The three camps were thought to represent Indians from different localities, Juneau, Yakutat, and Sitka. They were camped on the gravelly beach, just above high water, and for the most part occupied ordinary canvas wall-tents, though some few lived in the square bark-covered shelters which in ancient times were their summer homes. These shelters consist of a square frame of poles, loosely covered by strips of spruce bark, from a foot to eighteen inches

SHAMAN'S CARVED RATTLE AND STAFF.

wide and eight or ten feet long, laid on the framework, and held in place by slender poles placed over them. This bark must of course be brought from a distance,

PRIMITIVE BARK SHELTER, YAKUTAT BAY.

since trees large enough to furnish such bark do not grow in the neighborhood. At most of these bark shelters, skins of the hair seal still on the drying frames, were leaning against the wall, outside, and in some cases had been thrown up on the roof.

In the center of this shelter is the circle of stones forming the fire place, and over the fire, resting on the stones, is the pot full of strips of seal blubber, from which the oil is being tried out. The woman who watches the pot from time to time ladles out the oil into small kegs and old tin cans, or rarely into ornamented rectangular boxes of a primitive type. These boxes, as is well known, are made in three

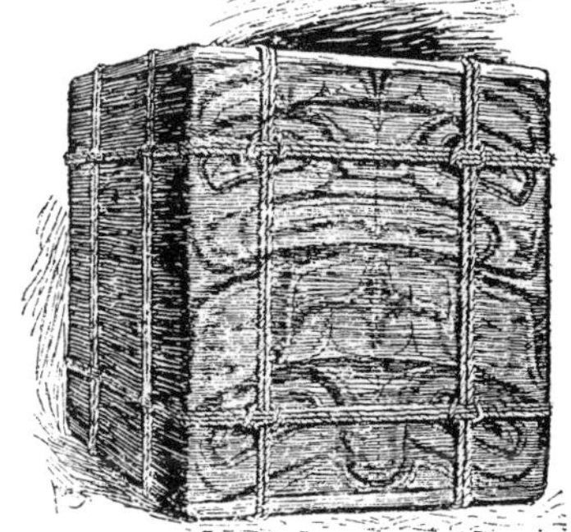

OIL BOX.

pieces, the cover, the bottom, and the sides. The thin plank which forms the sides is cut part way through in the line where the corners are to come, and is then steamed and gradually bent, and at last when the opposite ends come together to form the fourth corner of the box, they are fitted in a tight joint and sewed together with twigs or sometimes with cedar bark. Such boxes were once universally employed to hold oil, but at present their use has been largely superseded by articles of white manufacture.

From the poles which support the roof of the shelter hang delicacies of various sorts, all from the hair seal's body. There are flippers, sides of ribs, strips of blubber and braided seal intestines. All these things are eaten; and, in fact, during this fishing the Indians must subsist chiefly on the flesh of the seal. The flippers appear to be regarded as especially choice. We saw many women roasting them over the fire. After they were cooked the women pulled them out of the ashes, and heating an iron in the fire singed the hair which remained on the skin and then tore the flippers to pieces and picked the meat from the bones. Here was seen a primitive form of kettle, common perhaps to all North American tribes; it was a large seal skin, laced by its margin to a square frame of poles, hanging down in the middle eighteen inches or two feet, and full of strips of blubber; it would hold from one to two bushels.

The process of 'butchering' the seals absolutely reverses the method common in other regions. The product sought for is the blubber, which is attached to the hide. This being the case the Indian woman does not skin her seal, but opens it by a long gash along the belly and cuts out from the inside of the hide the meat and the bones, leaving the blubber attached to the skin. The flippers are cut off, the legs, the ribs, and loins taken from the

PHOTOGRAPH BY CURTIS JOHN ANDREW & SON

INDIAN SEALERS' CAMP, YAKUTAT BAY

body and put to one side, and the remainder, consisting of head, backbone, and attachments, lifted out of the skin and thrown away upon the beach. All the cutting is done with a broad crescent-shaped knife of iron or stone, the back of which, if of iron, is set in a rounded wooden handle, in which a thumb hole is sometimes made. When a woman has removed half a dozen seal skins, she kneels on the ground behind a board which she rests against her knees, and spreading the hide, hair side down on the board, rapidly strips the blubber in one large piece from the hide, which as she draws it toward her is rolled up by a twisting motion into a thick rope. The great sheet of pinkish-white blubber is then cut into strips and put to one side, to be tried out a little later.

FLENSING SEAL HIDE, YAKUTAT BAY.

The Indians kill the seals not for the flesh, although this is eaten, nor for the hides, though these are used, but for the oil, which is a necessity to them. They drink it, preserve berries in it, and use it for cooking, so that it really forms a considerable and important part of their food. The month of June, therefore, is usually spent in Yakutat Bay, on what is perhaps the greatest hair sealing ground on the coast. When the Harriman expedition reached that point there were between three and four hundred people gathered there to secure the annual supply of oil.

The seals are hunted in small canoes, usually occupied by two persons. They are light, and until one has become accustomed to them, seem cranky and likely to tip over. The shape of the cutwater is peculiar, for under the prow the wood is cut away backward, and beneath this again projects forward just above the water's level, with the result that this projecting point of wood first

YAKUTAT SEALING CANOE.

strikes and pushes away the ice cakes which so thickly float upon the water's surface, and prevents them from battering and chafing the bows of the canoes.

The two seal hunters in the canoe may be two men, or a man and his wife, or a man and boy. The hunter sits in the bow and his companion in the stern, while amidships are placed three or four large stones for ballast, weighing in the aggregate 150 or 200 pounds. Each occupant sits or kneels on a little platform fitted into bow and stern, or perhaps on a pile of branches covered by a blanket, a coat, or a skin, so as to keep him above the water, of which there is always more or less in the canoe. To the right of the bowman, and so of course immediately under his hand, are his arms, usually a Winchester rifle, or double-barrel shot gun, and a seal spear ten or twelve feet in length. Sometimes the hunters wear white shirts and hats, made of flour sacks, and sometimes white cloth is hung over the gunwales of the boat, so as to make it seem like a piece of floating ice. This precaution is less commonly employed where ice is abundant, as in Yakutat Bay, than in places where there is less ice. Many of the bergs here are covered with dirt, and are of all shades from white to black. Much of the surface of the upper end of Yakutat Bay is covered with floating ice which is continually falling from the fronts of the glaciers which pour into it, and it is among this floating ice that the sealing is done. The hunters paddle along slowly, keeping a sharp lookout for the seals. When one is observed they sit still, but as soon as it dives they paddle as swiftly as possible toward the spot, continuing their efforts until it is almost time for the seal to reappear. They are so familiar with the habits of the animal that they can gauge the time very closely.

SEALER'S HUTS OF DRIFTWOOD, GLACIER BAY.
HUNYA INDIANS.

SEALER'S HUT, YAKUTAT BAY.

When the seal is about due at the surface the paddlers stop and look for him, the hunter holding his gun in readiness to shoot. If the seal appears within range the shot is fired, and if the animal is wounded both men paddle to him as fast as possible, and the hunter tries to spear him, either by throwing or thrusting with the spear. A long, light line is attached to the shaft of the spear near its head, and the end of the line is retained in the boat. The spear point, being barbed on one side, seldom or never pulls out, and the seal is dragged to the side of the canoe, struck on the head with a club, and taken on board. If the first shot should have merely wounded the seal, and it is impossible to spear him, he is pursued and shot again whenever he

HUNYA SEALER'S CAMP, GLACIER BAY.

comes to the surface. Few seals are lost unless they can get among the thick ice where the canoe moves with difficulty, and the floating blocks interrupt the view. When a seal is taken into the boat an equivalent weight of stones is thrown overboard to lighten the canoe. Often before noon the canoe has all the seals that it can carry, and returns to the camp.

When the village is reached women help unload the canoe and carry the seals up the beach, while the men take the boat up above high-water mark.

It would be difficult to form a close estimate as to the number of seals killed by these Indians, but more than 500 skins were counted in the camp where we spent most of our time, and it would seem that a thousand seals would not be too large a number to be credited to the three camps that were located near the head of the bay.

For many generations this has been a sealing ground for the Indians, and in some places the beach is white with weathered bones and fragments of bones that represent the seal catches of many years. The surroundings are not attractive, for the place resembles a slaughter-house. The stones of the beach are shiny with grease; seal carcasses and fragments of carcasses are spread along the shore, and there is an all-pervading odor of seal and seal oil. The place is a busy one. Back of the beach is a lagoon of fresh water, from which the Indians get their drinking water, in which the children wade about, sailing their canoes, and in which the mothers bathe their babies.

North of Yakutat Bay no Indians were met with, all the natives seen from that point onward being Aleuts or Eskimo.

DEATH'S HEAD CARVINGS.

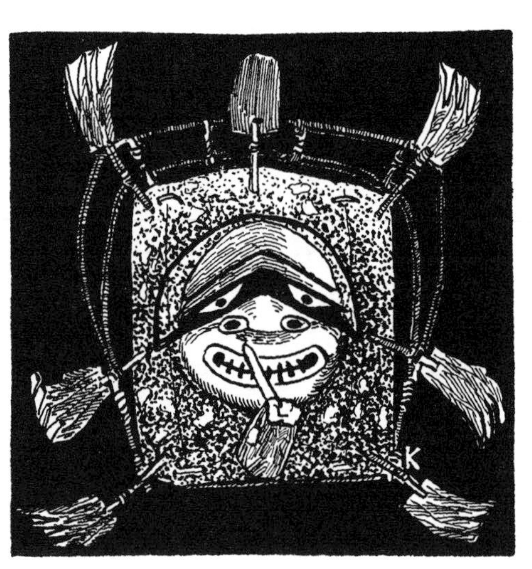

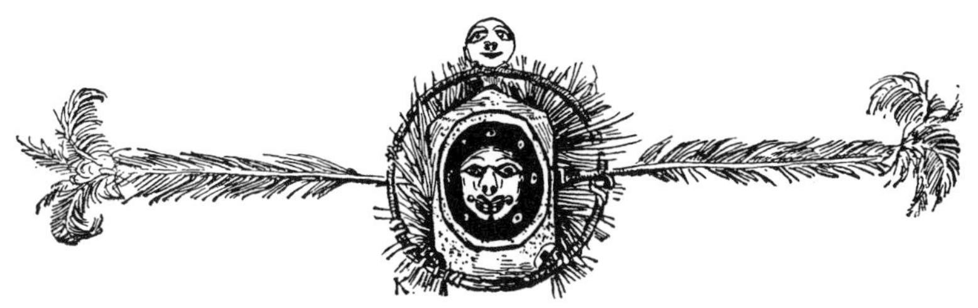

THE ESKIMO WE SAW

It was at Prince William Sound that the Harriman Expedition saw the first Eskimo. According to Dr. Dall, the native people of Kadiak, the eastern end of Alaska Peninsula, and Cook Inlet down to Copper River, are genuine Eskimo and speak a dialect closely like that of the Arctic Eskimo and quite different from that of the Aleuts. The Aleuts do not come farther east than the Shumagin Islands. We first met them at Unalaska; afterward at the Pribilof Islands.

At the present day the Aleuts are supposed to number less than 2,000 people, though the old navigators who discovered their existence gave them a population of from 25,000 to 30,000, which seems not unreasonable when we consider the conditions of their life in their primitive estate, and the abundance of their food supply. These people are of Eskimoan stock, but the separation of the two branches must have been long ago for they speak a language which the Eskimo do not understand. Their traditions are so similar to those of the Eskimo, and the implements which they used in primitive times so much the same that there is no longer any doubt about their relationship.

The Aleuts have long been under the influence of the Russian Church, and have largely abandoned their primitive ways. They are now Christianized and in a degree civilized. They are a hard-working people, but nevertheless find it difficult to gain a subsistence under the changed conditions which surround them, and the increasing scarcity of the wild creatures on which they used to depend for food. At Unalaska all the laborers are Aleuts, as are also all those employed in the fur-seal fisheries on the Pribilof Islands.

The name Aleut was applied by the Russians to the inhabitants of the Aleutian Archipelago as well as to the

BIDARA OR ALEUT SKIN BOAT, ST. PAUL ISLAND, BERING SEA.

inhabitants of Kadiak Island and the southeast shores of the Peninsula of Alaska. Dr. Dall believes that at one time, until driven out by the Indians, these people also occupied the north shore of the Alaska Peninsula. He believes further that the Aleutian Islands were populated at a very distant period, and that those who first occupied them were more like the lowest grades of the Eskimo than to the Aleuts of historic times; and that while the development of the Eskimo went on in the direction in which it first started, that of the Aleuts was modified and given a different direction by the conditions of their surroundings. Population entered these islands from the eastward, that is, from the continent, and little by little spread along the chain of islands. Many hints as to the change and development in the people and their ways of life have been found by Dr. Dall in the shell heaps which he has so carefully studied, and on which he has reported so fully and so entertainingly.

The Aleuts of to-day are not only greatly changed from their primitive conditions by the partial civilization forced on them by the Russians during the period of their occupation, but they are also modified by a considerable infusion of Russian blood due to that occupation.

Away from the settlements, however, they still live somewhat in their old fashion, and at the remoter villages, such as Kashega, Chernofski, and Akutan, occupy the barábara, an oblong, rectangular house with vertical walls only two or three feet high, with a roof sloping up to a height of about six feet, where it becomes flat again. Such houses are from twelve to fifteen feet wide, and from eighteen to twenty long; the door is in one end, and in the middle of the flat roof is a smoke hole, two feet long by 18 inches wide, immediately above the fireplace. At a distance of about four feet from the side walls of the house a stout pole is laid on the ground for the whole length of the structure; between this pole and the wall the ground is covered with hay or straw, forming the sleeping places. At the back of the house and thus opposite the door, in several of these houses that I entered, was a small altar, bearing a cross, and before it a

BARABARA OR NATIVE ALEUT HOUSE AT UNALASKA.

low wooden box or platform on which the worshipper might kneel. Practically all of these Aleuts belong to the Greek Church, and conform to its outward observances. The barábara is built of wood, sometimes of planks neatly joined together, or again of strips of cottonwood, roughly split out and fitted as closely as possible. Over this foundation of wood is a thick thatch of dried grass, held in place by heavy sticks laid upon it, which in turn are bound down with withes of willow. Sometimes the covering is merely this thatch, or it may be overlaid with earth and sod, on which grows a rank vegetation. The buildings are warm, dry, and comfortable, and it is stated that flies and mosquitoes never enter them. This is no doubt explained by the fact that when occupied they are extremely smoky.

A THREE-HATCH BIDARKA.

Away from the few settlements, the Aleuts still depend entirely on fishing and on the chase. The population is sparse, and the country is divided into districts for fishing and for hunting—each district belonging to certain families and handed down from father to son. No Aleut trespasses on the territory of his neighbor, either for fishing or hunting. Near the mouths of certain salmon rivers visited, we found the barábaras belonging to the owners of the fishing there, and even their drying scaffolds, and some of their fishing implements hung up against the time when they should return, in the season when the salmon are running.

The Harriman expedition's view of the Aleuts was, of course, hasty and superficial. It does not appear worth while to repeat here what has been written by explorers whose opportunities for studying them were so much better than ours.

PHOTOGRAPH BY MERRIAM

Eskimo alongside ship

PHOTOGRAPH BY DEVEREUX JOHN ANDREW & SON

Plover Bay, Siberia

Our next view of northern peoples was at Plover Bay in Siberia, which the ship reached a day or two after leaving the Pribilof Islands. Here was found an Eskimo vil-

ESKIMO SUMMER HOUSE AND FIREPLACE, PLOVER BAY, SIBERIA.

lage, apparently long established; it consisted of half a dozen topeks or summer houses, and a greater number of winter houses, most of which were then unroofed and dismantled, and either empty or used as storehouses for casks of oil, skins, sledges, drying frames, and a variety of articles not in present use.

ESKIMO WOMEN AND CHILDREN, PLOVER BAY.

The inhabitants of the village numbered perhaps thirty, about twenty men and women and ten children. They were now occupying their summer houses, which were roughly circular in shape, and consisted of vertical walls formed of poles set in the ground, about which skins were stretched, and covered by a roof of skins which sloped up to a blunt point not far back of the door. The walls were perhaps eight feet high and the apex of the roof ten or even twelve. On the roof the skins came together but did not fit closely, so that there was abundant room for the smoke to escape, though there was no actual smoke-hole. The cooking is done mainly with oil and does not produce much smoke.

The door of the summer house in this village is rather wide, and sometimes so high that one may enter without stooping. The fireplace stands to the left of the door, and about it is a circle of large stones. Casks and kegs, which hold meat and oil, stand close to the walls beyond the fireplace, while to the right of the door are boxes, trunks, and sealskin bags which contain other property. From poles which run from point to point overhead are hung tools, implements, lines, and drying meat and hides.

The family sleeping apartment is cut off from the rest of the hut; it stands well back from the door and is protected from any rain that may leak through the roof by a tightly stretched green walrus hide fastened above it near the roof, and slightly inclined backward. Four poles set in the ground at the four corners support a frame of four other slender poles from which hang the walls of the sleeping tent. This is rectangular, perhaps twelve feet from one end to the other, six feet deep, and six high in front, but only about five at the back. The tent is com-

PART OF ESKIMO SETTLEMENT, PLOVER BAY.

PHOTOGRAPH BY CURTIS JOHN ANDREW & SON

ESKIMO WINTER HUT, PLOVER BAY, SIBERIA

posed of reindeer skins, dressed soft, but with the hair on, the hair side being out. The front wall is loose at the sides, and lifts up. The family when retiring to rest, lower the front curtain, and usually sleep quite naked. Sometimes the tent is divided in the middle by a partition, but usually there is none.

UNFINISHED WINTER HOUSE, SHOWING FRAMEWORK OF WHALE BONES.

In many respects the winter houses are similar to those used in summer, but are larger and more substantial. They consist of a circle of upright posts which stand a foot or two apart. The posts are straight whale ribs planted in the ground and projecting six or eight feet. Between the uprights are piled one upon another sods wide enough to fill the gap, and reaching up to the top. This of course makes a solid wall, quite impenetrable to cold. From the top of this wall the poles which support the roof, which is not greatly inclined, run together at the apex. As in the summer house, the poles are covered

WINTER HOUSE COMPLETELY SODDED BUT LACKING ROOF.

with dried, stretched hides of walrus and the great seal. These houses are warm and comfortable, but of course close and smoky. As soon as the weather grows warm in spring the people move into the summer houses and pull the roofs off the winter ones, sometimes taking down the sods as well, so that the interior of the winter houses may be exposed to sun and wind, and may dry.

All through the village, on poles and frames, hung the various property of the inhabitants — deer skins, some of them of the domesticated Siberian reindeer obtained by trade from the Chukchis of the adjacent interior, others of the caribou or wild reindeer of the American coast; on drying frames were spread the skins of seals and walruses, while scattered all about were seal nets, inflated seal bladders, the inflated complete skins of seals, turned inside out and drying — to be used as walrus floats, or perhaps as oil cans, or perhaps merely as sacks in which to transport property. Standing or hanging against the sides of the houses were harpoons, spears, and paddles; seal nets made of slender strips of rawhide — sealskin — while between the posts, all about the village, were stretched great lengths of seal and walrus hide, cut into slender lines, to be used for making dog harness, for lines to be attached to the harpoon when hunting, and in making seal nets. Three or four bone frames were seen, formed of the curved ribs of the whale, which reminded one somewhat of one of the Plains sweathouses. Under each one of these there had been a fire, and under one the fire was still burning and a pot was boiling over it.

ESKIMO MAN AND WOMAN, PLOVER BAY.

It was apparent that this village had been occupied for a

very long time. All about it lay the mouldering bones of whales, and eight whale skulls in various stages of decay were counted.

At various points in and near the village were seen old pits dug in the gravel of the bar, in which at times blubber is perhaps stored until it can be tried out. In other words, the pits are storehouses, though in this climate, where in the shade at least it is always cold, it would hardly seem that refrigerators were required.

It was interesting to note that in the case of one of the summer houses, and one of those used in winter, the door was closed by setting up against it the shoulder blade of a small whale. The same bone is sometimes used as a table.

The men of this village seemed hardy, sturdy, and about as tall as the average man, but particularly robust above the waist. The women, on the other hand, were quite short. One middle-aged woman near whom I happened to stand would not have come up above my armpit. At this village I saw no women of average height. The men were erect, free walkers, and rather graceful; the women were quite the reverse, walking with an uncertain shuffle, and often bent forward. The men all had the crown of the head shaved, the hair being cut short all about in a tonsure. All had scanty beards and mustaches. Several of the older women appeared to be tatooed on the chin,

ESKIMO MAN AND WOMAN, PLOVER BAY.

cheeks, and forehead. These marks are said to be made by running under the skin a needle to which is attached a thread of sinew which has been blackened by charcoal.

All these Eskimo were dressed in clothing of reindeer skin. The parkas or shirts worn by the men usually have a collar of bear or wolf fur and are short, ending about at the waist. The women's parkas are long, usually hanging down to the knees. The men wear leggings, more

ESKIMO WOMEN, PLOVER BAY.

or less tight fitting, and reaching to the knee. The women wear extremely large and baggy knickerbockers. Both sexes use the common sealskin mukluks or boots, which reach to the knees. The children of either sex dress like the adults.

These Eskimo live altogether on flesh, hair seal, walrus, whales, and ducks furnishing them their chief support.

About a mile from the village, under the high bluff which seems too steep to be climbed by man, is the village burying ground. Soon after dissolution the dead are carried to the gravelly beach at the foot of this bluff, where, dressed in their ordinary clothing, they are laid on the ground and left. The dogs of the village soon devour them, all except the skulls, which roll about until destroyed by the weather.

In this village we saw an old man wearing in his cheeks the ivory labrets which all the Eskimo used to wear.

Better than any description that can be given of the village and its people are the reproductions of photographs, taken by the expedition, which accompany this account.

ESKIMO BELLE, PLOVER BAY.

It had been proposed to stop, after leaving Plover Bay, at Indian Point, where there is another Eskimo village, but when the ship reached there, late in the night, it was found that the surf was so heavy that no landing could be made. It had been hoped also that it might be practicable to stop at King Island, a vertical rock opposite Port Clarence, inhabited by a village of very primitive Eskimo.

They occupy caverns in the cliffs, and reach and leave their homes from stagings built out over the water on poles fastened into the rifts in the rock. It is said that it is impossible for them to land on the island in stormy weather; although they can drop into their canoes at such a time, they cannot get from them. The King Island Eskimo are reported to be of great stature, and the men to wear labrets. The women are said to equal if not excel the men in size and strength. It is also said that here in a deep cavern running back from the canyon there is a great bank of perpetual snow, which the Eskimo use for storing their meat and fish, which thus is preserved indefinitely. The King Island village is said to be a large one, consisting of nearly 200 people. Although the ship passed within sight of the island it was unfortunately not found practicable to visit it.

PLOVER BAY ESKIMO.

At Port Clarence, the next point visited after leaving Plover Bay, a large number of Eskimo were found encamped on the beach, having come there to trade with the whalers and to hire out to them for the coming cruise in the Arctic. When we reached our anchorage, several Eskimo umiaks came out to us to trade, and before long ten of these great boats containing, according to a count by the mathematician of the ship, more than 175 persons, were alongside. The boats were bright yellow, the color of the dried skin, and were filled with people, some

ESKIMO DISH CARVED FROM VERTEBRA OF WHALE.

clad in skins and some wearing red or blue shirts. The bottoms of the boats were covered with sealskin bags, mingled with deer skins, dogs, and babies. The only silent and impassive living creatures in the vessels were the dogs and the babies; all the others were holding up the articles they wished to trade—hides, bits of carved ivory, mukluks or skin boots, and walrus teeth, and all were shouting at the tops of their voices. It was a scene of great confusion. Most of what they offered to sell was not worth buying, since they had undoubtedly parted with all their best things to the whalers. The members of the ship's company gave exorbitant prices for some very worthless things, and paid chiefly in silver, most of which unquestionably soon found its way on board the whalers, to be traded there for spirits. After a time the Eskimo left the ship to return to the beach, and soon the party landed and spent some hours wandering through their camps.

ESKIMO UMIAK.

There was a continuous camp of natives stretching all along the curving beach for a mile or more. Some of these had come from Cape Prince of Wales, others from Cape Nome, and others still from St. Michael. Most had recently arrived, and their property was not yet

ESKIMO KAYAK.

unpacked, but was lying on the beach just as it had been removed from the boats. Each camp had at least one large umiak or skin traveling boat, and there were a few kayaks. The Eskimo were well provided with food; they had fresh seal and walrus meat, dried seal meat, fresh salmon and smelts, and large quantities of dried flat-fish. They had also buckets filled with tiny, silvery fish, somewhat like a smelt in general appearance, but very small. These they were eating and also feeding to the dogs.

These Port Clarence Eskimo were a stout, sturdy people, and all of them seemed strong and healthy. Among them were several quite tall women, one at least of whom overtopped most of the men and boys about her. All, men, women, and children, seemed healthy, and all seemed quite clean.

ESKIMO WOMAN, MAN, AND CHILD, PORT CLARENCE.

Each family had at least a half dozen dogs, which were usually tethered on the beach by twos and threes. While some of them were white and others black, most were gray and very wolf-like in appearance. I have never seen dogs that looked so much like wolves. They all seemed very good-natured, and not at all disposed to regard strangers with suspicion. Scarcely any of them barked at the members of the party who were strolling around among them.

The hunting implements that these people carry were many of them of primitive type — harpoons, seal spears, and fish spears, tipped with ivory or bone. I saw one

Eskimo baskets, Port Clarence, Alaska

Photographs by Curtis John Andrew & Son

Aleutian baskets, Atka Island, Alaska

particularly fine bundle consisting of a large harpoon, two shorter spears, a fish spear, and some spear handles. Not many stone tools were seen, partly, perhaps, because they had not unpacked their possessions. One man, however, had a fine chisel of jadeite, and we came across two stone pipes of the old type. They possessed a few baskets of good form and quality, of the Point Barrow type. They had one or two adzes made from an ordinary lathing hatchet, the head having been taken off, turned half round and then lashed to the handle so as to form an adze.

ESKIMO STONE PIPE.

In the piles of packages on the beach were seen many of the sealskin bags in which they carry their possessions. Some of these were made from the skin of the ribbon seal, others of the ringed seal, and others still, of the common Pacific harbor seal. These, skinned out through the mouth, with no other cut in them, and tied up at both ends, are used for a variety of purposes: they serve for whale floats or for oil casks, or, when completely dry, tanned, and turned right side out, for dunnage sacks. When used for this purpose a slit is commonly cut across the breast, from flipper to flipper, and this is laced up.

Most of these Eskimo had set up ordinary wall tents of canvas or muslin with a low wall and door, so that to enter it was necessary to get down on the ground and creep under the wall. There were a few oval frames of willow twigs covered with canvas; and in two or three cases an umiak propped up on its side supported the upper edge of a sheet of canvas which was pinned to the ground below.

Planted in the soil behind several of the tents were

sticks surmounted by small, rudely carved figures, usually painted black or white, or black and white. One of these figures represented a bear, another a bird; on another the figure of a man and a woman stood on either side of a circular piece of wood on which were painted concentric rings, so that it looked somewhat like a rifle target. The man who was standing by the tent to which this figure belonged explained that this was 'all same sun.' Our means of communication were not sufficient to learn just what he meant by this, but the figures were unquestionably sacred emblems of some sort.

ESKIMO WOMAN, SHOWING CUT OF PARKA, PORT CLARENCE, ALASKA.

The parkas of the men and women here differed noticeably: the women's had a long scallop hanging down in front and behind, while the men's were of equal length all around, and reached down only a little below the hips. The men had the crown of the head shaved, while the women's hair hung loose or was carelessly braided at either side. Many of the children were very pretty and clean, free from shyness, and disposed to make friends.

Here at Port Clarence one or two Eskimo were seen wearing a wolf or dog tail hanging down from the belt behind. This reminded us of the report made by Popoff, long a captive of the Tchukchis in Siberia, nearly 200 years ago, when he told the Russians that he had heard that beyond the sea, to the east, there was a great land inhabited by people who had tusks growing out of their cheeks, and had tails like dogs. The old man seen at Plover Bay had labrets in his cheeks, which were these tusks, and here at Port Clarence were the men who had tails like dogs.

The outlook for the immediate future for these Eskimo is gloomy. Hitherto they have been well cut off from civilization, meeting only the whalers, who are few in number and are under a certain rude discipline. But a change has come for the Eskimo and this year of 1900 has already witnessed a melancholy alteration in their condition. The rush to the coast gold fields has brought to them a horde of miners, who, thinking only of themselves, are devoid of all feeling for others of their kind. There is no law or government in the land, the commanders of the few revenue cutters along the coast being the fountain heads of authority and having extensive areas of sea and land under their jurisdiction. White men, uncontrolled and uncontrollable, already swarm over the Alaska coast, and are overwhelming the Eskimo. They have taken away their women, and debauched their men with liquor; they have brought them strange new diseases that they never knew before, and in a very short time they will ruin and disperse the wholesome, hearty, merry people whom we saw at Port Clarence and at Plover Bay.

Perhaps for awhile a few may save themselves by retreating to the Arctic to escape the contaminating touch of the civilized, and thus the extinction of the Alaska Eskimo may be postponed. But there is an inevitable conflict between civilization and savagery, and wherever the two touch each other, the weaker people must be destroyed.

THE SALMON INDUSTRY

BY GEORGE BIRD GRINNELL

THE fisheries of Alaska constitute one of its greatest economic resources, but they have been little exploited, except so far as the salmon are concerned. There are half a dozen species of salmon, not all of equal value.

Spending most of their time in the salt water, the salmon in summer run up the fresh-water streams as far as they can, and there deposit their eggs. Many of them die before they return to the salt water; many others are destroyed by enemies of one sort and another, and it is commonly believed by the local fishermen that after a salmon has deposited its spawn the question of its death is one of a very short time only.

SALMON WHEEL, COLUMBIA RIVER.

The world's output of canned salmon comes chiefly from our Northwest coast. In 1897 this output is said to have been not far from 3,000,000 cases, with forty eight one-pound cans to the case. Of this, Alaska produced about 1,000,000 cases.

In most salmon streams the fish appear to be about the same size and age. All the females are likely to be very similar in appearance; all the males also resemble each other. There are, however, exceptions to this rule; that is to say, some streams are entered by more than one species.

The spawning ground sought by the salmon is usually sandy or gravelly bottom in a pool or eddy, but sometimes beds are swept out and spawn is deposited where the bottom is covered with stones, varying in size from a hen's

SALMON DRYING.

egg to a man's fist. During the winter the eggs of the salmon hatch out, and in the spring after the ice passes out of the lakes the young salmon move down the streams and can often be seen at the mouths in large numbers.

It is an astonishing sight to witness the ascent of a small salmon stream by the fish, urged on by the reproductive desire. They work their way slowly up over riffles, where there is not nearly enough water to float them, but they seem to have the power of keeping themselves right side up, and so long as it does not fall over on its side, a fish six or eight inches deep can wriggle over shoals where the water is not an inch deep nearly as fast as a man can run. On such a stream one may catch in his hands great salmon weighing ten or twelve pounds, or may kick them out on the bank with his feet. And while the appearance of a man in the shoal water will at once alarm the fish and send them darting in all directions, up or down the stream, or even out on the bank, yet they soon return, and begin again to work their way slowly up through the shallow water.

If one inquires of an individual connected with the salmon industry in Alaska something about their numbers, he is at once told of the millions found there, and informed that the supply is inexhaustible. The same language will be used that was heard in past years with regard to the abundance of the wild pigeons, or of the buffalo, or of the fur-seals of Bering Sea. But if the investigator will continue his inquiry, and ask for the details of today, he will learn that it now takes far longer to secure a given number of fish than it used to, and that the fishermen are obliged to travel much farther from the cannery than formerly to secure their catch. As the reserve of the new acquaintance wears off and he becomes interested in his subject, what he says will show very clearly that the supply of Alaska salmon is diminishing, and diminishing at a rapid rate.

The salmon in the early summer come up from the deeper waters toward the mouths of the fresh water streams, and for some weeks may be seen in the bays, inlets, and fiords collecting in great numbers, preparatory to running up the stream. At this time they may be taken in considerable numbers in such places by trolling with the hook and line, and afford good sport. At morning and evening they are seen in numbers leaping out of the water, sometimes fifteen or twenty following one another, all leaving and entering the water almost at the same place, as if chasing one another.

When the fish have at last congregated at the mouths of the rivers, the work of the canners begins. They seldom cast their nets unless fish are actually seen, but when the salmon are visible the seine, from three to five hundred fathoms long, is swept through the water, and the captured fish are loaded on to the steam tug, which then takes them to the cannery.

The fishermen who manage the small boats and sweep the nets are either Indians or Aleuts. The crews of the steam tugs are usually white men, while the workmen on the wharf and in the cannery proper are all Chinamen, except for an occasional foreman or skilled mechanic.

After the loaded tug is tied up to the wharf, two or three men equipped with single-tined forks toss the fish from the deck to the wharf above, where they are received by other men similarly equipped, who pass them along to the gang who clean the fish at a long table. The man at the end of the table seizes a fish and cuts off its head and slides it along to the next man, who by two rapid cuts along the back takes out the backbone and loosens the entrails. It is then pushed on to the next man, by whom these loose pieces and whatever blood there may be in the visceral cavity are scraped away, the tail is cut off and the fish is thrown into a tank of water. From this it is lifted and placed with many others in a large tray, which is wheeled into one end of the cannery building. All these operations have taken place on the wharf, without the cannery and over the water, so that usually all the waste products fall down into the water below, where a part is devoured by the trout, which are constantly to be seen swimming about, a part by the gulls and other birds which congregate in great flocks near at hand, and the remainder is swept back and forth by the tide, much being carried

PHOTOGRAPH BY CURTIS

JOHN ANDREW & SON

At Lowe Inlet, British Columbia

away, but enough left on the beach to give the place a decided odor of its own.

The tray of cleaned fish is placed at the end of a long machine, where a carrier belt, divided into compartments about 18 inches square, by wooden partitions standing at right angles to it, is constantly ascending at an angle of about 40° to the top of the machine, which is ten or twelve feet above the floor. This belt is formed of short boards linked together. The board cross partitions are not continuous, but have two or three divisions wide enough to permit heavy knives to pass down through them. Above the belt, not far from the top, is a cam in which are set a number of large knives, and this cam, revolving at the same rate with the movement of the belt, sends down a set of knives through each compartment as it moves along.

As the belt moves on, a single fish is placed in each compartment, is carried upward, is cut by the revolving knives into one-pound pieces, and when the compartment reaches the point where the belt turns to pass downward again, the fragments of the fish are thrown out on a table. All this machinery works automatically.

From the elevated table where the pieces of the fish lie, another carrier belt runs down toward another table. This belt is just wide enough to hold the one-pound fragments of fish, each of which is to fill a can. A man standing by the upper table keeps placing the pieces of fish close to each other on the belt, and they are carried downward to a point where there is a great rammer just large enough to fit into a one-pound can. This rammer works constantly back and forth across the belt carrying the fish. Opposite the rammer is a horizontal belt carrying a row of open empty cans, the mouths of which lie toward the inclined belt which carries the fish. The tin cans move at such a rate that the mouth of one is opposite the rammer at each forward motion that it makes, and at each forward motion a one-pound fragment of salmon is jammed into an empty can, the can is carried on, and another empty can follows it, into which another piece of fish is thrust. This goes on without interruption, minute after minute and hour after hour, so long as the supply of fish holds out.

The belt carrying the filled cans now throws them out on a wide flat table surrounded by men, one of whom sets them on end as he receives them from the machine. Those that are completely full are whirled across the table to a man who with a cloth wipes the grease or moisture or salmon flesh from about the open end of the can, in order that when the cover is soldered on, the solder may take proper hold of the tin. Those not quite full are thrown to another man, at whose right hand is a pile of bits of salmon flesh. He fills the can and pushes it along to the wiper. The latter, as soon as he has finished with the can, slides it across to another who places a fragment of tin on the contents in such a position that it will be under the middle of the cover, which is now put on by another man, standing near the end of the table. The filled and covered cans are constantly gathered up and placed in trays by two men, who carry them across a short passage and set them down near a man who is attending to the soldering machine. They are laid side by side on a belt which runs down to a metal trough just as wide as a can is high and deeper at one side than at the other, the lower side being full of molten solder. The trough and solder are kept hot by a blast beneath them. The cans are moved forward by means of a heavy chain hanging over them. The belt carries the cans down to this trough. The edge of the cover where it meets the can rolls along for ten or twelve feet through this molten solder, then the can passes on to another belt, is tipped so that it stands on its bottom and rides along on the belt to a point where men stand with trays ready to gather up the cans and carry them over to the testers, whose business it is to determine whether the cans are absolutely air tight or not. For this purpose a large number of cans are set in a strap-iron crate, which is lowered into a tank of water. If bubbles rise from any can, it evidently is not tight, and is removed and another one put in its place. In this way five, ten, or twenty cans may be taken from the crate, which is then lifted out and carried over to the great boilers, into which crates full of cans are rolled and where they are cooked by steam for an hour.

The defective cans are passed over to the solderers and by them carefully examined; the holes are soldered up by hand and the cans then go back to the testers.

After the cooking process the cans are gone over again to see whether any are defective, and then are stacked up in great piles on the floor. From these piles they are taken to racks, ranged over tanks of shellac, and when one of these racks is full, by a simple device its contents are dipped into the tank beneath, lifted out, and left there to drain. The shellac soon dries; then the cans are removed from the rack and again stacked up on the floor, where the final operation of putting on the labels is performed. When this has been done they are ready for casing, forty eight one-pound cans going into a case.

The salmon of Alaska, numerous as they have been and in some places still are, are being destroyed at so wholesale a rate that before long the canning industry must cease to be profitable, and the capital put into the canneries must cease to yield any return.

This destruction of salmon comes about through the competition between the various canneries. Their greed is so great that each strives to catch all the fish there are, and all at one time, in order that its rivals may secure as few as possible. With their steam tugs, their crews of white men and Aleuts, and their immense seines they first sweep the waters near the canneries, and then, when these have been cleared out, go further and further away, until at present many canneries, having exhausted the nearby waters, are obliged to send their tugs 60 or 70 or even 100 miles to find fish for the pack. The fish are caught with seines, some of which are 300 fathoms long, some 450 fathoms, and I was told of one 750 fathoms long and 18 to 20 feet deep. These seines are run out near the mouths

ALEUTS DRYING SALMON AT UNALASKA.

of the rivers where the fish are schooling preparatory to their ascent, and of course everything within the compass of the net is caught. Not only are salmon taken by the steamer load, but in addition millions of other good fish are captured, killed, and thrown away. At times also it happens that far greater numbers of salmon are caught than can be used before they spoil. A friend told me of the throwing away of 60,000 salmon at one time near a cannery in Prince William Sound in the summer of 1900, and again of the similar throwing away of 10,000 fish. At these particular times the salmon run happened to be very heavy, and more were caught than could be consumed by the cannery. So something like 700,000 pounds of valuable fish was wasted.

One of the best known salmon districts of Alaska may be chosen as an example of what this wasteful method will do for any river. I was told recently by a person very familiar with the canning industry and with Alaska that the catch of salmon in the Kadiak and Chignik districts — which put up nearly 44 percent of all the Alaska canned salmon — for 1896 was nearly 360,000 cases; for 1897 it was about 300,000 cases; for 1898, 90,000 cases, and that up to midsummer in 1899 the fishing had been practically a failure. And what is going on in the Kadiak district is going on in other districts. Competition is so very sharp between the great canning companies, as well as between the smaller individual concerns which run canneries, that each manager is eagerly desirous to put up more fish than his neighbor. All these people recognize very well that they are destroying the fishing; and that before very long a time must come when there will be no more salmon to be canned at a profit. But this very knowledge makes them more and more eager to capture the fish and to capture all the fish. This bitter competition sometimes leads to actual fighting — on the water as well as in the courts. A year or two since, one company which was trying to stop another from fishing on ground which it claimed as its own, sent out its boats with immense seines, and dropping them about the steam launches of its rival tried to haul them to the shore. This action led to long litigation, which resulted in a verdict for the company attacked.

Thus the canners work in a most wasteful and thoughtlessly selfish way, grasping for everything that is within their reach and thinking nothing of the future. Their motto seems to be, "If I do not take all I can get somebody else will get something."

Congress has passed laws governing the taking of salmon in Alaska, but they are ineffective and there is scarcely a pretense of enforcing them. It is true that each year inspectors are brought up on the revenue cutter to see that the law is obeyed, and of course these in-

SALMON BARRICADE.

spectors see very clearly that it is violated in every direction. Where the violations are so flagrant that they force themselves on the inspectors' notice the canners are told that they are doing wrong, and that the violations of the law must cease. The canners reply to them, "Yes, we know you are quite right; it is wrong. We do not wish to do as we are doing, but so long as others act in this way we must continue to do so for our own protection. Speak to our rivals about this. We will stop if they will."

The rival companies, when spoken to, make the same reply; so accusations are bandied back and forth. Nothing is done and the bad work goes on.

Nor are the concerns satisfied with capturing the vast quantities of fish as they are schooling in the salt water preparatory to running up the streams to their spawning ground. To do this systematically would be to catch most of the fish, but it would not catch them all — it would not make a clean sweep. So, on many of the streams the companies build dams or barricades, designed to prevent any fish from ascending. Drawn by instinct to the mouths of the rivers, the fish crowd to them trying to ascend, pushing forward, going only in one direction, and never becoming discouraged so long as life remains. None ever turn back, and so, in the course of the summer the whole number which in the natural course of things would ascend a river finally collect at its mouth. If the nets are systematically drawn, all these fish are caught; not one escapes, and the river is absolutely despoiled of breeding fish for that year. Not one ascends, and so no eggs are deposited and no fry are hatched the next spring.

Of course this absolute obstruction of the streams is practicable only on the smaller rivers. But it is carried on to a greater or less extent all through the Territory wherever it can be done, and yet "the erection of dams, barricades, fish wheels, fences or any such fixed or stationary obstructions in any part of the rivers or streams of Alaska . . . is declared to be unlawful," and is punishable by a fine not exceeding $1,000 or imprisonment at hard labor for a term of 90 days, or by both such fine and imprisonment, and by a further fine of $250 per day for each day that such obstruction is maintained.

There are certain rivers too large to be barricaded, and up these some fish run, notwithstanding the continual netting at their mouths. Such rivers often head in considerable lakes, where the fish spawn. It is the common practice of many of the canners to fish with nets in these lakes, and with an utter disregard for consequences to catch the fish while occupied in depositing their eggs.

As the natives of Alaska, many of them Aleuts, subsist largely on salmon, the regulations of the Treasury Department permit them to fish for food, and they are not subject to the general law which provides "for the protection of the salmon fisheries of Alaska." Advantage is taken of this liberty still further to destroy the fish. The natives catch all the salmon they wish and sell them to the canners, and this goes on indefinitely wherever the prohibition against fishing is in any degree regarded. Of course the natives, ignorant of the law, and, like the white man, eager for present gain, are glad to catch the fish and to sell them.

It must be remembered that long before the white man had come to Alaska, the fisheries on most of the streams resorted to by the salmon already had owners. For hundreds of years the Indians and the Aleuts had held these fisheries, not in the general way in which an Indian tribe claimed to possess a certain territory, but with an actual ownership which was acknowledged by all and was never encroached on. Their rights to the fisheries were as real as to the arms that they bore or the boats in which they traveled. For centuries certain families or certain clans had held proprietary rights in particular streams, and they alone could take fish from them. No Indian would fish in a stream not his own. He respected the rights of others, just as he expected others to respect his own. These ancient rights have now been taken from the natives by force, but they are still anxious to get what they can from the fishing.

On some streams it is easier to take the fish in traps than it is to stop them by means of barricades, and then

PHOTOGRAPH BY U. S. FISH COMMISSION

JOHN ANDREW & SON

SALMON DRYING AT CHERNOFSKI VILLAGE, ALEUTIAN ISLANDS

net them from the water below the barrier. In such places traps are built with wings and low dams up which the fish can pass into a pool or lake, which at its head is dammed by an impassable barrier. When the pool is full, or nearly so, it is swept clean by the net and left empty to be filled again. Thus all the breeding fish of a season may be and often are caught.

I was told that one of the great corporations established in Alaska had received permission to establish a fish

CAMP OF NATIVE SALMON FISHERMEN, KADIAK ISLAND.

hatchery, and that the employees of this company during the day catch fish ostensibly to strip for the hatchery and at night take them back to the cannery and can them.

It is well remembered that the island of Afognak, lying just east of Kadiak Island, and in one of the richest salmon regions of Alaska, was set aside some years since by Presidential proclamation as a forest reserve. Formerly there was a cannery on this island, but it has been discontinued and the machinery moved away. This, however, does not make much difference in the destruction of the salmon. The streams of Afognak Island are constantly fished by means of nets and barricades, and this reservation, like some of those within the limits of the United States, is a prey to whoever may be the first to despoil it.

Within a few years there has sprung up in Alaska a new and particularly wasteful method of using salmon. This is the salting of the bellies. It is perhaps not generally known that the most delicate part of the salmon is the belly. In old times certain tribes of Indians — where the fish were sufficiently abundant — habitually cut out and dried for their winter food the bellies alone, throwing away the remainder of the fish. In various parts of Alaska the same practice is carried on to-day. Only the bellies of prime salmon are preserved, salted, and packed in barrels for shipment, the whole fish, except the belly, being thrown away. In other words only from 10 percent to 20 percent in weight of each fish is used, the remainder being wasted.

Very little capital is required to establish a saltery. All that is needed is a rough shelter from the weather, salt, barrels, and labor. On the other hand to establish a cannery requires some money, for the buildings must be of a permanent character, and more or less elaborate machinery is required. A saltery may be established almost anywhere, and may readily be moved from one place to another. The salted bellies are recognized in the market as choice food and bring good prices. Thus almost anyone may establish a saltery and the business offers especial attractions to men of small means.

Salting is practiced at various points in Alaska, one of the best known salteries being situated near Tyonek on Cook Inlet. At this particular place king salmon — known in British Columbia and the United States as 'chinook' salmon — are used. These are the largest and choicest of the Pacific coast salmon, but they are destroyed as unthinkingly as any of the others. At other salteries the varieties known as humpback and cohoe also furnish bellies for salting.

This practice may fairly be compared with the old time method of killing buffalo for their tongues alone, and the more recent one of killing elk and deer for their hides or heads or hams. It should be stopped; but even if forbidden by law there is no hope that in the present condition of governmental affairs in Alaska the law would be other than a dead letter. When — if ever — matters in Alaska shall have become so settled that the taking of salmon shall be under governmental supervision the salting of salmon bellies, like many other abuses existing there, will be put an end to.

By the law passed June 9, 1896, now in force, entitled "An act to amend an act entitled 'An act to provide for the protection of salmon fisheries of Alaska,'" it is specifically provided:

1. That streams shall not be dammed or barricaded nor traps used on them to prevent or impede the ascent of the salmon to their spawning grounds, and that the Secretary of the Treasury shall establish and enforce such regulations as may be necessary to insure compliance with the provisions of the law relating to salmon fisheries of Alaska.

2. That salmon shall not be taken except with rod or spear above the tide water of any stream less than 500 feet in width except for purposes of propagation; that nets and traps may not be laid or set for a distance of more than one-third the width of such rivers nor within 100 yards of any other net or seine in said rivers; that no fish may be killed, except in Cook Inlet and Prince William Sound, between midnight on Friday and 6 o'clock in the

morning of the Sunday following; that no salmon may be caught in any manner or by any appliance, except by rod or spear, in any stream less than 300 feet wide between 6 o'clock in the evening and 6 o'clock in the morning on each day of the week.

3. That the Secretary of the Treasury may set aside certain streams in which no fishing may be permitted, and that he may establish close seasons to limit the duration of the fishing season, or may prohibit the fishing entirely for one year or more.

4. The appointment is authorized of three inspectors of fisheries and their salaries are named.

5. Penalties for violation of the provisions of this act are announced.

As has been said, the law in force is entirely inadequate, but it is easier to see where it fails to protect than it is to suggest amendments which shall make it efficient. Persons in Alaska interested in canneries have expressed the opinion that a tax should be laid on the output of each cannery, and that this tax should be used to support hatcheries by which the supply of salmon in the streams might constantly be renewed. It is obvious that Congress, which enacts the laws, can know but little, or nothing, about the actual necessities of the case. The present law, which provides for the appointment of three inspectors to look after a territory one-fifth as large as the whole United States, where there are no means of transportation and where every stream that is six inches deep is a salmon stream, is entirely inadequate, and in fact authorizes the throwing away of the small amount of money that is paid to each of these men. Many of the provisions of the present law are excellent so far as they go, and the chief weakness lies in the fact that no means are provided for enforcing the statute.

It is obvious that the expense of enforcing the law protecting salmon in Alaska should be borne by those who are engaged in the business of catching and selling these salmon. The canners should be taxed presumably on the output of their factories, and the revenue received from this source should be used from year to year for the purpose of restocking the streams and protecting them. It might be practicable also to lease certain streams to cer-

SALMON DRYING BY ALEUTS.

tain companies on reasonable terms, not permitting them to fish except on the streams that they have leased.

What has already been written concerns the summer of 1898 and previous seasons. Since then, there appears to have been no material change in the conditions, except that the summer of 1900 was marked by an unusually good run of salmon in certain rivers, and that certain catches were large.

The report of the Special Agent of the treasury for 1900, which become accessible while these pages were passing through the press (April 1901), shows that violations of the law by the methods already described continue, and while this agent takes a most cheerful view of the prospects of the fisheries and declares that many new canneries are being established — a condition which is likely always to follow a year in which there has been a good run — yet an inspection of his report indicates steady and continuous diminution in the numbers of the fish taken, and strongly emphasizes the importance of measures to increase the supply and protect the breeding fish. In describing the process of salmon taking and canning he says: "It is reported that with the help of steam power and the use of the largest size of seine as many as 75,000 salmon have been taken at a single haul. But that never happens nowadays, when a catch of 5,000 is accounted extremely good and very often a few hundred only are secured." These few words tell the whole story.

Some slightly increased interest appears to be felt in the direction of artificial propagation. The report implies that four practical hatcheries are in operation in Alaska, and says that their output of salmon fry will not exceed 14,000,000 — a number about equal to two-thirds of the annual catch. As only about one percent of these fry are supposed to mature, it is obvious that as yet the efforts to supply the annual loss caused by commercial fishing are entirely insignificant.

Notwithstanding the wholesale destruction which is thus going on, the salmon of Alaska are not in danger of actual extermination. Long before anything of this kind had taken place the canneries and indeed commercial fishing of every description would have been abandoned as unprofitable, and the streams — even those that had been most ruthlessly fished — would slowly reestablish themselves. But the selfish and shortsighted policy of taking everything in sight cannot fail to render unprofitable in a very short time the whole Alaska canning industry, and to make it necessary to abandon the costly plants that have been established at so many points. Even if the government is too indifferent to interfere to regulate the fishing, it would seem that as a mere matter of business policy the corporations and individuals interested in the industry would get together and devise plans for their own protection; but small jealousies and the fear of being overreached by competitors have hitherto prevented this.

The question of the protection of these fisheries is not one of sentiment in any degree. It is a question as to whether the material resources of Alaska are worth protecting. Beginning twenty years ago in a very small way Alaska has produced up to this time about 7,500,000 cases of salmon in addition to large quantities that have been salted — in 1897 15,500 barrels. The output of the salmon canneries according to the official report of the U. S. Treasury Department was in 1899 valued at $3,850,346; in 1900 $6,219,887. Certainly such a resource is worth saving and making perpetual.

Chas B Hudson

Index

References to illustrations are indicated in *italics.*